MICHIGAN!

Grace Kachaturoff
Professor of Education
The University of Michigan–
Dearborn

PEREGRINE SMITH BOOKS
SALT LAKE CITY

Table of Contents

95 94 93 92   5 4 3 2 1

© 1992 by Gibbs Smith, Publisher

Manufactured in the United States of America.

Design by J. Scott Knudsen

Library of Congress Cataloging-in-Publication Data
Kachaturoff, Grace.
    Michigan!

    Includes index.
    Summary: A history of Michigan's social, political, and ecomonic
growth with emphasis on the ethnic makeup of the state population.
    1. Michigan – History.   2. Ethnology – Michigan.
[1. Michigan – History.   2. Ethnology – Michigan]
I. Title.
F566.K23   1987   977.4   86-25986
ISBN 0-87905-228-7

Maps and Charts

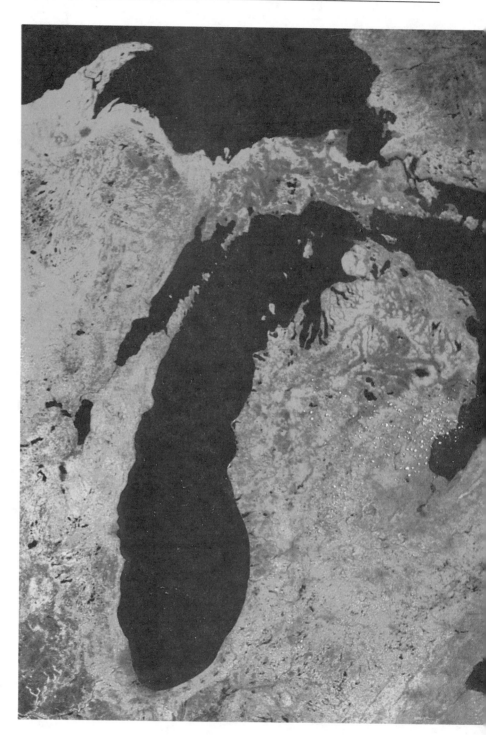

This is how Michigan looks from outer space. Can you identify the lakes in the picture?

Introduction

What Michigan Means

The word *Michigan* means "the land of the great lakes." It comes from two Chippewa words: *mithcaw* meaning "great" and *sagiegan* meaning "lakes." These words describe one of Michigan's important *resources:* its great and mighty waters.

Studying About Our State Community

The story of Michigan is the story of our state *community*. To know about our community will help us to understand ourselves and plan for the years ahead.

There are many ways to learn about our state. We can talk to our parents, grandparents, and friends about life in earlier times. We can read books and newspapers and watch films about Michigan. In these and other ways we can learn how our state came to be like it is today.

Social Scientists

Social scientists are people who study the earth and its people. There are many kinds of social scientists. *Historians, geographers, anthropologists,* and *archaeologists* are some. Each one has a special way of looking at people, things, and events.

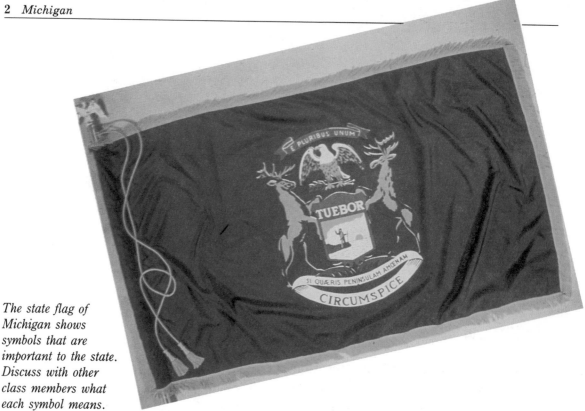

The state flag of Michigan shows symbols that are important to the state. Discuss with other class members what each symbol means.

A historian is a person who is interested in what people have done in the past. The historian studies written records, photographs, songs, and *artifacts* (things made by people). If a historian writes about something that is happening now, this is called an eye witness report. A historian may ask people what they remember about earlier years. What the people remember and tell is called *oral history*.

The geographer studies the earth's *climate* and *natural resources* and how people and animals use the earth. The natural resources are those things from nature which people and animals use. Some of these are coal, oil, trees, and water. The anthropologist studies people, their way of life, and how they live together.

The archaeologist studies *fossil* remains and artifacts to learn about life in the past. Fossils are hardened traces or remains of plant or animal life.

Many communities in Michigan have historical museums like these in Presque Isle (left) and Kalkaska (right). Do you have a historical museum in your city or town?

By studying what these social scientists have learned, we can come to know the history of our state and its people.

COMPARING HISTORIES

ACTIVITY

Pretend you are a social scientist from another planet. You have just reached earth in a spaceship. As you look around, you find a copper coin, a piece of glass, a sheet of paper with writing on it, and a rusty fork. What could you say about people on earth by studying these artifacts? Remember, you know nothing about earth life.

Do your classmates agree with your ideas? Why or why not?

Michigan's Natural Resources

Michigan's land is made up of two large *peninsulas*. A peninsula is a piece of land reaching out into a body of water. The soil, climate, and plants of Michigan are different from place to place.

The sandy shores of Lake Michigan attract many visitors to our state.

Picnicking by a river is an enjoyable family activity.

Michigan's waterways are an important resource. They are used for shipping goods to different places for the state's industries and factories. People also use the lakes and rivers to fish, boat, and swim.

Michigan is rich in *minerals*. Copper, iron ore, salt, sand, and gravel are some of the minerals found in Michigan. Factories and builders use these minerals in great amounts.

Michigan's Human Resources

People are *human resources*. The Indians were Michigan's first human resources. They came to the Michigan area to hunt and fish. Years ago people came to Michigan to work in the mines. Others came to farm. Still others came to work in the lumber camps. Later people came to work in the factories.

Many people came to Michigan who spoke different languages. They belonged to different churches and had different colors of skin. They came for jobs and a better way of life. In return, they helped to make Michigan a great state.

INTERVIEWING SENIOR CITIZENS

ACTIVITY

Invite a senior citizen to your class. *Interviewing* a senior citizen is the same as having a talk with a friend, except that you will want to prepare some questions ahead. Perhaps you could tape record the interview.

As a class, make a list of questions to ask a senior citizen about our state. Examples:

- Were you born in Michigan? If not, why did you come here?

- What was your life like when you were ten years old?

- What did you study in school? Did you have a lot of homework? What kind? Who was your favorite teacher? Why?

- What was your first job?

- What did you do for fun?

- What events do you remember best?

The questions may be about food, clothing, family, school, or way of life.

After the interview, talk about the interesting things you learned about Michigan.

Michigan's Products

Human resources and natural resources come together to make Michigan's products. Our state is known worldwide for three things—automobiles and machinery, breakfast foods, and furniture. These are made in factories in different parts of the state.

Many farm products are also raised here. These include navy beans, peppermint, sugar beets, soybeans, cucumbers, blueberries, and strawberries. Cherries, apples, pears, peaches, and plums are grown in Michigan's orchards. Farmers also grow wheat, hay, and other grains. Other important farm products are turkeys, hogs, and beef cattle.

A major Michigan crop is cucumbers for pickling.

Almost everyone likes to pick and eat apples in the fall. Can you describe what a crunchy apple tastes like?

You now have an overview of Michigan's land and how people use it today. It wasn't always the same. In this book we will learn about changes that have taken place over hundreds of years.

WORDS TO KNOW

STUDY

anthropologist

archaeologist

artifact

community

fossil

geographer

historian

human resource

interview

mineral

natural resource

oral history

peninsula

product

resource

social scientist

WHAT DID YOU LEARN?

1. Why should we study our state?

2. How can we learn about our state?

3. How can social scientists help us learn about Michigan?

4. Name four of Michigan's important natural resources.

5. Why did people want to live in Michigan?

USING WHAT YOU HAVE LEARNED

1. How can your own family's story help tell the story of your community?

2. How do Michigan's natural and human resources come together?

3. Suppose you read two different reports about the first moon landing. How would you know which one was more correct? If you read different reports about the French fur traders in Michigan, how would you know which was more true? Why?

MICHIGAN'S PLACE IN THE WORLD

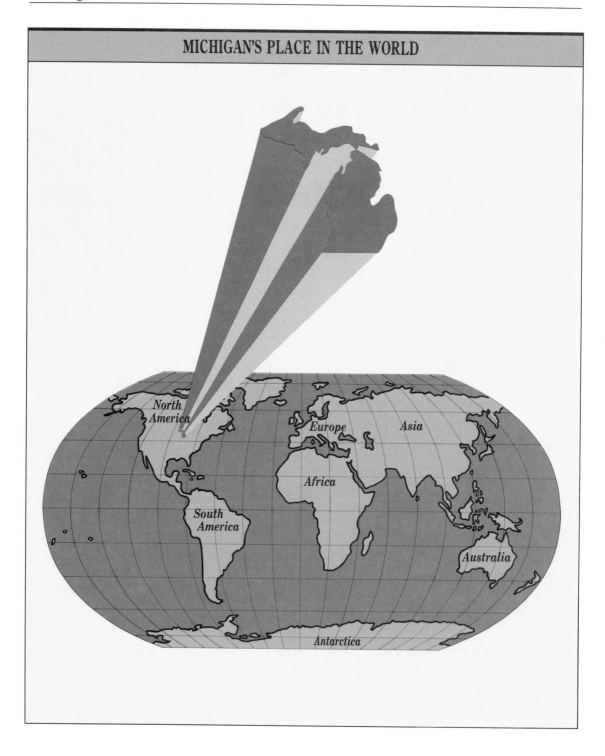

Geography: Mapping Michigan

What is Geography?

Geography is the study of the earth and its people. The way people live depends upon where they live and how they use the earth's natural resources. Forests, land, water, fish, and animals are some natural resources.

Geographers show us what they have learned on *globes* and maps. We can learn to use these tools to understand our world.

USING A GLOBE

ACTIVITY

Use a globe to find the United States. Tell about its location in different ways:

1. On which *continent* is Michigan found? (There are seven major bodies of land in the world, and they are called continents.)

2. Is Michigan north or south of the *equator?* (The equator is an imaginary line around the middle of the earth, halfway between the north and south poles.)

3. Name the countries and oceans which *border*, or touch, the United States.

Latitude and Longitude

Have you noticed other lines circling your globe? These lines help us to find places and measure distance.

Lines of *latitude* (LAT-ih-tewd) run east and west around the globe. They are numbered in *degrees,* measuring distance north or south of the equator. The equator is zero degrees latitude.

Lines of *longitude* (LON-jih-tewd) run from the North Pole to the South Pole. They measure distance east and west of the *prime meridian.* This is a line passing through Greenwich (GREN-ich), England. The prime meridian is zero degrees longitude.

FINDING MICHIGAN

ACTIVITY

Now let's find Michigan on the map of the United States on page 11.

1. In which part of the United States is Michigan located—northeast, northwest, southeast, or southwest?

2. What other states are found on the same latitude as Michigan? Do you think their weather, plants, or animals would be like Michigan's? Why or why not?

3. Which states border Michigan? Which country borders Michigan?

Describing Michigan's Geography

Michigan is a "water wonderland." Lake Michigan, Lake Superior, Lake Huron, and Lake Erie touch Michigan. These lakes, plus Lake Ontario, are known as the Great Lakes. Lake Superior covers 32,000 square miles. It is the largest freshwater lake in the world.

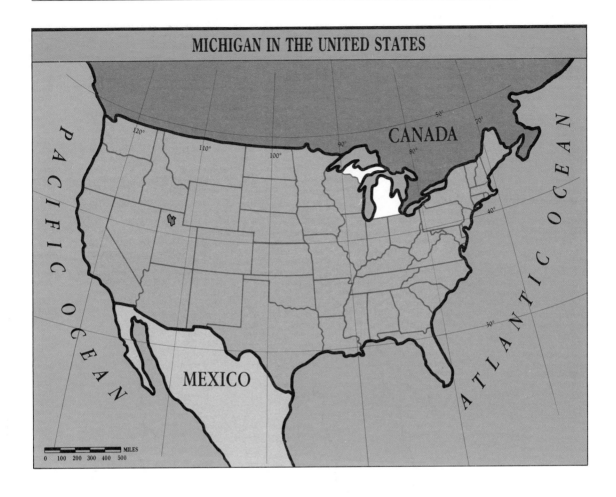

MICHIGAN IN THE UNITED STATES

Besides the Great Lakes, Michigan has over 10,000 inland lakes. These are valuable resources. Many people go there to fish, camp, and swim. Houghton, Orchard, Mullett, Higgins, Long, and Gull lakes are only a few.

Michigan also has many rivers. Some important rivers are the Detroit, St. Mary's, and St. Clair. These rivers connect the Great Lakes with the St. Lawrence Seaway, which leads to the Atlantic Ocean. Large ships from around the world use the St. Lawrence to reach Detroit and other cities on the Great Lakes.

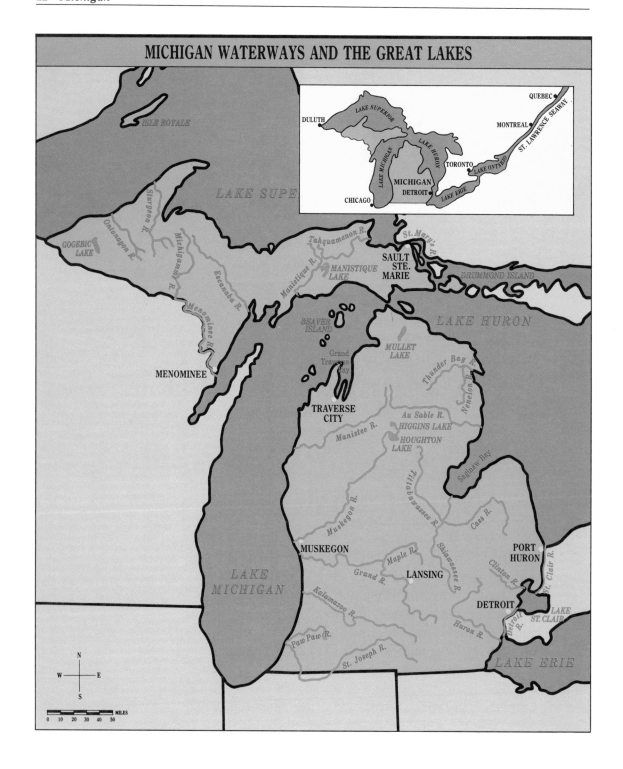

MICHIGAN WATERWAYS AND THE GREAT LAKES

ISLE ROYALE

LAKE SUPERIOR

DULUTH

QUEBEC

MONTREAL

ST. LAWRENCE SEAWAY

LAKE HURON

LAKE MICHIGAN

TORONTO

LAKE ONTARIO

MICHIGAN

CHICAGO

DETROIT

LAKE ERIE

LAKE SUPE[RIOR]

Sturgeon R.

Ontonagon R.

GOGEBIC LAKE

Michigamme R.

Escanaba R.

Menominee R.

Manistique R.

Takquamenon R.

St. Marys R.

SAULT STE. MARIE

DRUMMOND ISLAND

MANISTIQUE LAKE

BEAVER ISLAND

LAKE HURON

MENOMINEE

Grand Traverse Bay

MULLET LAKE

Thunder Bay R.

Nenelon R.

TRAVERSE CITY

Au Sable R.

HIGGINS LAKE

HOUGHTON LAKE

Manistee R.

Tittabawassee R.

Cass R.

Saginaw Bay

Muskegon R.

MUSKEGON

Maple R.

Shiawassee R.

PORT HURON

Clinton R.

St. Clair R.

Grand R.

LANSING

LAKE MICHIGAN

Kalamazoo R.

DETROIT

Detroit R.

LAKE ST. CLAIR

Huron R.

Paw Paw R.

St. Joseph R.

LAKE ERIE

N
W   E
S

MILES
0 10 20 30 40 50

Two Peninsulas

Two peninsulas make up Michigan's land shape. However, the total shape includes most of the Great Lakes. The map on page 14 shows all of Michigan's *boundaries.*

The two peninsulas are different. Most of the land in the Lower Peninsula is low and flat. In some places there are gently rolling hills and many small inland lakes. The eastern part of the Upper Peninsula is like that, too. But the western part has higher hills and some mountains covered with forests. The three highest mountains in the state are Brockway Mountain, the Huron Mountains, and the Porcupine Mountains.

In which part of Michigan can you find high hills and forest-covered mountains?

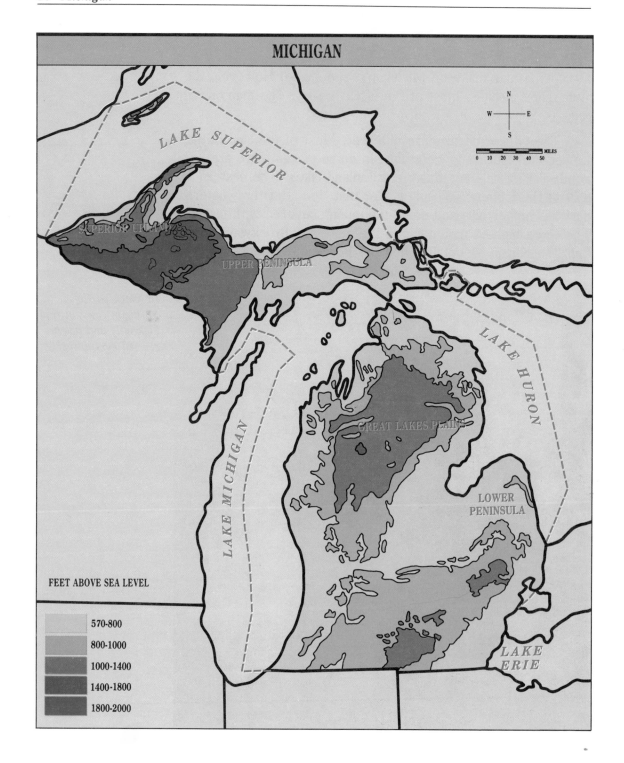

MICHIGAN

MACKINAC BRIDGE

The Mackinac Bridge connects the Lower Peninsula with the Upper Peninsula.

T*he Mackinac (Mak-uh-naw) Bridge, built in 1957, now connects the Lower Peninsula with the Upper Peninsula.* People can ride or walk on the Mackinac suspension bridge *from Mackinaw City across the* straits *to St. Ignace. It hangs from a thick steel cable stretched between strong towers. The Mackinac Bridge is five miles long.*

Understanding Maps

Maps are flat, and most are drawn to *scale*. That is, an inch on the map *represents* a certain number of miles on the land. For example, Detroit is 300 miles from Mackinaw City. On a map these cities might be just three inches apart. The scale would be 100 miles to one inch. Different maps use different scales.

Some maps have a *legend* of *symbols* and colors. The legend may tell us that blue represents water and green is forests. It may show certain symbols to represent things such as farm crops, oil wells, mines, or railroads. Always check the legend to find out what symbols are used on the map.

Maps help us find places, show directions, and measure distance between places. There are road maps which show how to get from place to place. There are maps to show the height of hills and mountains. These are called *elevation* maps. There are maps that show how the weather changes. Can you think of other kinds of maps?

Michigan's Land and Water Forms

Michigan is made up of different land and water forms. Lakes, rivers, oceans, and swamps are water forms. Land forms include hills, valleys, islands, and mountains.

Land and water forms are important to the people living in Michigan. They are also important to the plants and animals.

Michigan's Climate

Climate is the weather over a long period of time. Climate affects the *environment*. The average amount of rain that falls each year is enough for Michigan's water needs. There is enough to water farm crops and to take care of thirsty animals. There is enough for factory use and for watering

Michigan's climate is ideal for growing orchard crops. Michigan leads the nation in red sour cherry production and is third in the production of sweet cherries.

parks. Can you think of many more ways water is used in Michigan?

The Great Lakes play a part in the weather. The temperature of the lake water, the winds, and the amount of sunshine over the water are keys to weather changes. Along Lake Michigan's shore, the weather is ideal for growing orchard crops, such as cherries. Air above the lake stays cooler in summer than air above land. In winter the lake air is warmer than air over land. This keeps the temperature just right for fruit orchards.

TEMPERATURE AND RAINFALL

(Detroit) Lower Peninsula
(Sault Ste. Marie) Upper Peninsula

NORMAL TEMPERATURE

| | JANUARY | | JULY | |
	Maximum	Minimum	Maximum	Minimum
Lower Peninsula	32° F.	19° F.	83° F.	63° F.
Upper Peninsula	22° F.	6° F.	75° F.	53° F.

EXTREME TEMPERATURE

	HIGHEST	LOWEST
Lower Peninsula	105	– 16
Upper Peninsula	98	– 35

AVERAGE YEARLY RAINFALL

Lower Peninsula	30.96 inches
Upper Peninsula	31.70 inches

Source: National Oceanic and Atmospheric Administration, U.S. Department of Commerce

ACTIVITY

MAPPING MICHIGAN

Look at the map of Michigan on page 12. It shows some land and water forms.

1. Name the lakes which surround or touch Michigan.

2. Name the large inland lakes.

3. What are the biggest rivers?

4. Trace with your finger the Upper Peninsula and the Lower Peninsula.

5. Locate the eastern part of the Upper Peninsula. Locate the western part.

6. Most of the people in Michigan live in the south-eastern part of the state. Point to that area on the map. What are some possible reasons for this? Where do you live?

7. Point to Isle Royale, Drummond Island, Beaver Island, Grand Traverse Bay, Saginaw Bay, and Lake St. Clair.

Michigan Is Divided Into Counties

The state is divided into smaller sections called counties. County lines are imaginary. They cannot be seen on the land but only on maps.

Each county has a county seat. There the county buildings are located and county business takes place. Counties have their own police departments and courts, and they keep records. If you wish to know the history of your family's home or apartment, the records of it can be found at the county building. Births, deaths, and marriages are recorded at the county courthouse. Where is the county seat for your community?

There are 83 counties in Michigan. Most of the people live in four of them: Wayne, Oakland, Washtenaw, and Macomb. In which county do you live?

MICHIGAN COUNTIES AND COUNTY SEATS

KEWEENAW
1,900

Eagle
River

Houghton

HOUGHTON
38,200

Ontonagon

Ontonagon
9,400

L'Anse

LUCE
6,400

Bessemer

BARAGA
8,200

Marquette

Newberry

Sault Ste. Marie

GOGEBIC
18,600

IRON
13,700

MARQUETTE
74,800

Munising

CHIPPEWA
28,500

Crystal Falls

DICKINSON
26,100

ALGER
9,000

SCHOOLCRAFT
8,500

MACKINAC
10,100

Iron Mt.

DELTA
38,600

Manistique

St.
Ignace

Escanaba

MENOMINEE
26,000

EMMET
24,500

Cheboygan

Rogers City

Menominee

Petoskey

CHEBOYGAN
21,400

PRESQUE ISLE
14,200

Charlevoix

CHARLEVOIX
20,500

MONTMORENCY
8,100

Alpena

LEELANAU
15,100

Leland

Bellaire

ANTRIM
17,500

OTSEGO
16,100

Gaylord

Atlanta

ALPENA
31,500

Traverse City

Kalkaska

CRAWFORD
10,400

Mio

ALCONA
10,400

BENZIE
11,900

GRAND
TRAVERSE
58,900

KALKASKA
13,100

Grayling

OSCODA
7,300

Harrisville

Beulah

MANISTEE
23,300

WEXFORD
27,000

MISSAUKEE
11,000

Roscommon

OGEMAW
18,200

IOSCO
30,100

Manistee

Cadillac

Lake City

ROSCOMMON
18,900

West
Branch

Tawas
City

MASON
27,300

LAKE
8,600

OSCEOLA
20,200

Harrison

GLADWIN
22,300

ARENAC
15,600

HURON
36,100

Ludington

Baldwin

Reed City

CLARE
26,200

Gladwin

Standish

Bad Axe

Hart

White
Cloud

Big Rapids

ISABELLA
56,800

MIDLAND
76,200

BAY
116,200

SANILAC
41,400

OCEANA
22,900

MECOSTA
39,200

Mt.
Pleasant

Midland

Bay City

Caro

Sandusky

MUSKEGON
155,800

NEWAYGO
37,100

MONTCALM
50,200

GRATIOT
39,600

Saginaw

TUSCOLA
57,600

Muskegon

Stanton

Ithaca

SAGINAW
224,500

GENESEE
440,000

LAPEER
74,200

ST. CLAIR
141,200

Grand
Haven

KENT
464,000

Ionia

St. Johns

Corunna

Flint

Lapeer

Port Huron

OTTAWA
169,100

Grand
Rapids

IONIA
52,900

CLINTON
56,800

SHIAWASSEE
70,500

MACOMB
699,600

ALLEGAN
86,700

Hastings

EATON
94,900

INGHAM
276,100

Howell

Pontiac

Allegan

BARRY
48,100

Charlotte

Mason

LIVINGSTON
110,000

OAKLAND
1,029,100

Detroit

VAN BUREN
69,600

Kalamazoo

Marshall

Jackson

Ann Arbor

WAYNE
2,171,400

Mt. Clemens

Paw Paw

KALAMAZOO
216,900

CALHOUN
138,100

JACKSON
148,000

WASHTENAW
271,700

St.
Joseph

Cassopolis

Centreville

Coldwater

Hillsdale

Adrian

MONROE
135,500

BERRIEN
166,000

CASS
49,600

ST. JOSEPH
58,200

BRANCH
40,100

HILLSDALE
42,700

LENAWEE
89,700

Monroe

Total Population: 9,211,900

Figures from *Sales and Marketing Management,* July 28, 1986

LEARNING ABOUT COUNTIES

ACTIVITY

Study the map of counties on page 19. Then answer these questions:

1. Find your county on the map. What borders your county on the east, west, north, and south?

2. Which county seems to be the largest? Which looks the smallest?

3. Which two counties are the most crowded? Can you figure out why?

4. Compare the map of counties with the one on page 12. Which water forms are nearest your county? What land forms are nearby?

WORDS TO KNOW

STUDY

border
boundary
climate
continent
degree
elevation
equator
globe

latitude
legend
longitude
prime meridian
represent
scale
strait
suspension bridge
symbol

WHAT DID YOU LEARN?

1. What states border Michigan?

2. Which country touches Michigan?

3. Name the Great Lakes.

4. Why is Michigan's land shape not a complete picture of the state's size and shape?

USING WHAT YOU HAVE LEARNED

1. In what ways are maps useful?

2. When would a road map be more important than a land forms map? Why?

3. How do the Great Lakes affect the way you live?

PROJECTS AND REPORTS

1. Collect and show different maps of Michigan.

2. Look at the county's maps for your school land. Share the information you learn with your classmates.

3. Draw a map of your own county, city, or neighborhood.

These students are using special tools to hunt for fossils.

Michigan's Indian Heritage

Before the Coming of People

Our story of Michigan begins about ten thousand years ago. At that time there were no people living here. The land was the home of huge animals such as mammoths, caribou, mastodons, giant beavers, and wild hogs. Fossil remains of these animals have been found. Fossils of three whales have also been found in Michigan. How did these ocean-living whales get to Michigan? Perhaps they swam up the Mississippi River or St. Lawrence River. They might have passed through some lakes which have since dried up.

Careful work has uncovered a trilobite which lived thousands of years ago.

It took thousands of years for Michigan to become as we know it today. Huge ice caps, called *glaciers,* once covered the land. They formed in the north during a very cold time called the Ice Age. Over the years, the ice spread slowly south as it became heavier. The last glacier in Michigan dragged rocks, sand, and wood. The land was covered with ice and debris.

As the glacier melted, land and water forms in Michigan were changed again. Wide valleys were carved and lakes were formed where before there were none.

Later plants and small animals appeared in the forests, and fish were swimming in the waters. Over time, the animals we now know began to make their way to Michigan. The year when people first appeared in Michigan is not known exactly. But scientists think it may have been about 6,000 years ago.

Paleo-Indian Hunters, the First People

We call the earliest people of Michigan Paleo-Indian hunters. They used chipped stones as weapons to hunt large game

The Michigan Historical Museum in Lansing has many displays which show the history of Michigan in an interesting way. This display shows how Paleo Indians might have dressed in the winter. When do you think the Paleo Indians lived in Michigan?

animals. They also fished and gathered roots, nuts, and berries. Paleo-Indians moved around in search of food. They knew how to make fire. They also buried their dead in a certain way. Food and a few tools found in the graves seem to show that they believed in life after death.

It is not known when and how Paleo-Indians came to Michigan. Some people think they may have come from Asia, crossing the Bering Strait from Siberia to Alaska about 14,000 years ago. From there they traveled to Michigan and other parts of America. Perhaps they followed herds of buffalo.

These people did not have written records. Artifacts tell us something about their way of life.

Archaic People

About 4,000 years ago, another group of people appeared in Michigan. They are called the Archaic people. They also hunted, fished, and gathered roots, nuts, and berries. The Archaic people, though, began to stay in one place for a few months each year. Village life was begun. Like the people before them, they believed in life after death. Many copper tools, pieces of carved stone jewelry, and shells have been found. They seem to have been made just to bury with the dead.

It is believed that Archaic people were the first to discover and use copper in Michigan.

Woodland Indians

The Woodland Indians lived in Michigan from about 600 B.C. to the late 1600s. Woodland Indians also believed in life after death. They buried their dead under huge piles of earth up to 30 feet high and 200 feet around. They sometimes made large buildings atop the mounds. More than 600 *burial mounds* have been found in Michigan. For this reason, these people are also called Mound Builders.

Some Indian mounds are still being found today. Many of the mounds were destroyed by early settlers as they prepared the land for farming. Clinton County, northwest of Lansing, has the greatest number of mounds—57. In Lenawee County

Many burial mounds like this one can be found in Michigan.

51 mounds have been found, with 46 in Kent County and 33 in Saginaw County.

One mound was found inside the grounds of Fort Wayne in Detroit. Two miles south of Grand Rapids are the Norton Mounds. Mounds have been found near the Rabbit River in Allegan County, twelve miles from the mouth of Grand River in Ottawa County, and many other places in Michigan.

The Woodland Indians were Michigan's first farmers, raising corn and other plants. Farming meant they could have permanent settlements and stay near their burial mounds. They didn't have to move to find food.

Skilled workers made jewelry and clay pots. They wove cloth with thread made from tree barks. They carved tobacco

Native American Indians became very skilled at beadwork. They also did leather and wood crafting to make beautiful and useful things.

pipes in the shapes of people and animals. Woodland Indians traded with groups of people far away to get beads, shells, and metal for their workers.

Historic Indian Nations

Around 1640, when the first Europeans arrived here, there were about 15,000 Indians living in both the Upper and Lower peninsulas. Indians from this time on are said to be *historic* because there are written records of them.

An Indian nation was made up of many families who were related to each other. They believed the same things and spoke the same language. The three major groups were the Chippewa, Ottawa, and Potawatomi. They called themselves the "three fires" and were friendly toward each other.

The Ottawa, Chippewa, and Potawatomi belonged to the Algonquian language group. So did some smaller nations—the Miami, Menominee, and Wyandot. The Hurons belonged to

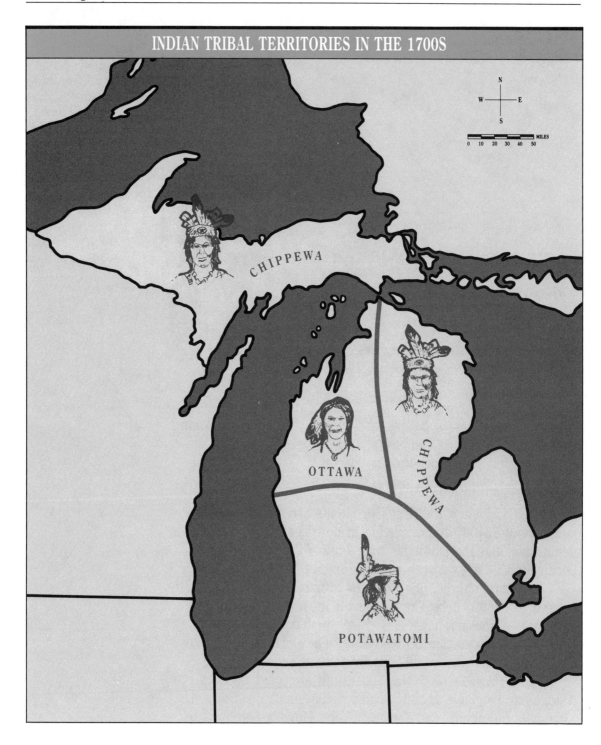

INDIAN TRIBAL TERRITORIES IN THE 1700S

CHIPPEWA

OTTAWA

CHIPPEWA

POTAWATOMI

N
W   E
S

MILES
0 10 20 30 40 50

the Iroquoian language group. The Hurons and the Ottawas lived peacefully together even though they belonged to different language groups.

Indians kept on the move searching for food and furs. This meant that nations lived in different places in Michigan at different times.

Chippewa Way of Life

The Chippewa lived in *clans* (family groups) of 5 to 25 families.

Men and women had certain jobs to do. During the summer months, men hunted small game and fished with hooks, spears, and nets. Whitefish was a favorite catch. Women did the cooking. Along with the children and elders, women also gathered nuts, roots, berries, and honey. The women sewed clothing for the family, set up camp, and took care of the children.

This painting is by the famous American artist Frederick Remington. It shows a Native American storing a deer for later use.

In autumn the men hunted for deer, moose, beaver, and other animals. Until the Europeans came, bows and arrows and traps were the chief weapons. Beaver was hunted for its meat and fur. Beaver skin was used for trade and for clothing.

A *ceremony* for good luck began every hunt. Hunting was not a sport. If the hunters failed, families might starve without meat for the winter. Families also stored wild rice and corn for winter use.

The Chippewa built fine canoes. After the Indians got tools from the French explorers, they made the canoe even stronger and lighter. A light canoe was easier to pick up and carry from one river to another. The canoe was a great way to travel in Michigan with its many rivers and lakes.
The Chippewa, like the other groups, believed in helping others. They willingly shared whatever food they had.

Ottawa Way of Life

The Ottawa lived in bark-covered lodges in the northwestern part of the Lower Peninsula. They were good traders. Trading for things they did not have was common among Indians. The

Dugout canoes were made by burning, then scraping out large logs.

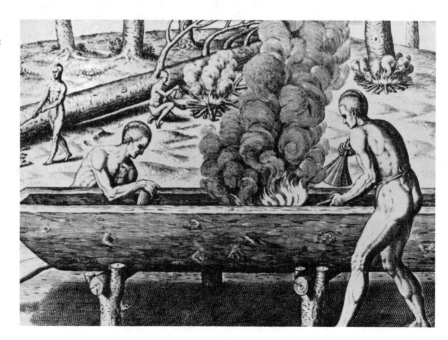

Ottawa grew a large part of their food in their gardens.

Potawatomi Way of Life

The Potawatomi were also good farmers. Potawatomi means "people of the place of the fire." They cleared land for crops by burning the grass and bushes.

They lived on *fertile* lands near rivers. The women planted corn, squash, beans, melons, pumpkins, and tobacco. Tobacco was used as an offering to the spirits. The men hunted and fished. Like the Chippewa and Ottawa, the Potawatomi gathered sap from maple trees. The women boiled it to make syrup and sugar for their own use and to trade with others.

The Potawatomi moved into the forests during the winter for hunting and to protect themselves from winter winds.

Things Tribes Had in Common

The Indians did not believe in owning *private property,* as we do. For example, the men hunted together and the meat was divided among all the families. It did not belong just to the hunter who killed the animal. The land belonged to everyone. Indians cared about everyone in the group. They would give away what they had to someone else who needed it.

When anyone was ill, the medicine man was called. He sometimes used medicines made from roots, leaves, or seeds. Some people today find that some Indian medicines are good cures and have scientific support.

When Indians moved, the women carried all their possessions. The men had to be free to defend the group from enemies. The men also hunted food for their meals. The women gathered the wood, kept the fire going, and brought the water. For meals, the women made stew, roasted meat, and baked bread and seed cakes.

Indians were good builders and woodworkers since there was plenty of wood. They made many woodworking tools. From trees they built homes, made canoes, and carved dugouts. They made bows and arrows, oars, and spoons. The women also made baskets and bowls from tree bark.

A wigwam covered with mats.

Homes and Clothing

The Indians made dome-shaped homes for the winter. A framework of *saplings* was covered with large sheets of tree bark. The Chippewa sometimes built *wigwams* for summer use. They wove mats of cattails and long grasses for roofs and walls.

Snowshoes and toboggans helped Indians get around in winter. Skins of buffalo, bear, and beaver were sewn into heavy blankets.

The women wore loose blouses and skirts which they made from animal skins. They *tanned* the skins, then cut and sewed them into clothes for the whole family. Men and women wore leggings and moccasins. The women also wore lovely jewelry made of beads, shells, and copper.

Making snowshoes. Why were snowshoes so important?

Indian Leaders

The Indian chief was the most important person in the group. A leader had to be wise and brave. He had to be a good hunter, fisherman, and speaker. Men earned the honor of being chief. Other men and women were also leaders in the Indian nation.

SHINGAUBA WOSSIN, CHIPPEWA CHIEF

Shingauba Wossin was an important leader among the Chippewas. He was the first chief of the Chippewa nation at Sault Ste. Marie. He was respected by both Indians and whites for his common sense. He wanted people to live in peace. An important treaty was signed by him in 1825. A treaty is a written agreement between nations that they will live in peace and do certain other things. This treaty ended the wars among the Indians. Chief Wossin signed another treaty which promised education for Indian children.

Because early Indians did not write, they had other ways to make treaties with Indians, white settlers, and governments. They used *wampum* (a string of small beads) and the *calumet* (a long-stemmed pipe). The colored beads could be arranged in different ways on a belt. Each pattern meant something different. When a matter was decided, the calumet was brought in, filled with tobacco, and lighted. Then it was passed around the group. This meant the people present promised to follow through on the deal they had just made.

Belief in Gods

Religion was important to all Indian groups. The Indians believed in many gods, or spirits. They believed that spirits lived in everything: people, plants, animals, rocks, thunder, rain, and sun. Some of the spirits were good, others bad. If a man wanted to have a good hunt, he would offer gifts to a certain spirit that ruled over hunts. If Indian farmers wanted to have good crops, they would also offer gifts to the spirits.

The Ottawa believed that Nanabozho was one of the great spirits who lived in the sky. He sometimes visited his home on Mackinac (MAK-uh-naw) Island. He was the spirit who had taught Indians how to catch fish by using nets.

Changes in the Indian Way of life

Indian life changed after the 1600s. It was then that European fur traders and settlers began to affect the Indian ways. Little by little Indians began to depend on others for food and tools. They no longer made bows and arrows. Instead they traded with the Europeans for guns and hatchets. They made fewer baskets and pots because they could buy these things.

The Indians spent little or no time in farming because Europeans wanted furs. The Indians could trade furs for European goods. So they hunted animals for trade, not food.

Lack of food, poor health, and white people's diseases soon took lives of hundreds of Indians.

This painting by Robert Thom shows a trading post. There Indian families traded furs for goods they needed.

Treatment of Indians

Indians often were not treated fairly or honestly by white people. Their lands were bought cheaply by the settlers or were taken from them. The settlers wanted the lands for their own farms. They tried to force the Indians to move to other states. Some Indians escaped to Canada.

Four *reservations* where Indians could live were set aside in Michigan by the United States government. These lands often were not as good for farming and hunting as lands the settlers had taken for themselves. Today Indians may choose whether or not to live on a reservation.

The Indians were *native*-born Michiganians. Yet, they were not granted the rights of citizenship until 1924. They would like to be treated fairly and enjoy all the freedoms that other Michigan citizens have. Indian groups are working to improve life for their people. They hope to get jobs and better housing for Indians today.

Indian Contributions

The Indians have made many *contributions* to the American way of life. The canoe is one. Many people still use canoes on Michigan's rivers. Some people use snowshoes to hike around the hills and mountains in winter. Old Indian trails have become the routes for our major highways and roads.

Indians gave us many foods for our diet. Corn became an important food for the hunters and early settlers. We still enjoy it today. By living off the land, Indians have shown that people can live in harmony with nature.

We have used many Indian words to name our rivers, cities, lakes, and other places. *Michigan* is an Indian word. Can you list some other Indian names you have heard or seen in Michigan?

Indian leaders have given us some fine examples to follow. They have shown us how to live in peace with each other. They have been brave and wise.

Arrowheads were chipped from hard stones like flint or obsidian. The arrowheads were often tied to wooden shafts with thin strips of rawhide.

HENRY R. SCHOOLCRAFT, 1793-1864

H enry R. Schoolcraft was a geologist. *He helped explore the Upper Peninsula and the Mississippi River in 1820. Because of this trip, he became very interested in Indians. He studied their way of life and wrote many books* about them.

Schoolcraft became an Indian agent at Sault Ste. Marie in 1822. Later he became Superintendent of Indian Affairs for all of Michigan. He served in that job from 1836 to 1841.

At this Indian Basket Market in Mackinac, a variety of handmade goods is being offered for sale. The photograph was taken around 1900.

CHIPPEWA LEGEND

A legend is a story that is passed down from generation to generation. Often each person the story changes it a little, so it may or may not be all true. A Chippewa legend collected by Henry Schoolcraft told about the origin of the red-breasted robin. A part of the religious observance among the Chippewa was "fasting," when no food was eaten. If the fasting was completed properly, the guardian spirit would bring glory and prosperity.

An ambitious and vain father had one son who was of age to make the final fast. The father wanted his son to be better than anyone else in the tribe and directed him to fast for more days than anyone else.

The son was obedient and did as his father wished. After the son visited the sweating lodge and bath, his father told him to lie down on a mat for twelve days in a special lodge. Then he would receive food and the blessing of his father.

Each day his father visited and encouraged the boy to continue fasting, for great wisdom and honors would soon be his. On the ninth day, the son spoke for the first time and asked his father's permission to break the fast and do it another time. The father would not listen and encouraged his son to continue. The son agreed. On the

eleventh day he repeated his request; again the father ignored him. The boy was weak. The father told him he would himself prepare the son's first meal for the twelfth day.

When the father approached the lodge on the last day, he heard his son talking to himself as he painted his breast red. The son was saying that his father had ruined him because he would not listen to his request. His father would now be the loser. The guardian spirit took pity on the unhappy young man and changed him into a beautiful red-breasted robin.

He flew to the highest pole and told his father that he would still cheer him with his songs for the loss of the glory he had expected. The robin would forever bring peace and joy to the Chippewa.

WORDS TO KNOW

STUDY

burial mound	glacier	tan
calumet	historic	traditional
ceremony	nation	treaty
clan	native	wampum
contribution	private property	wigwam
fertile	reservation	
geologist	sapling	

WHAT DID YOU LEARN?

1. What major things helped shape Michigan's land?

2. From where did the first people in Michigan likely come? Why did they come to Michigan?

3. How do we learn about Indian life before the 1600s?

4. Name three Indian groups who lived in Michigan before the 1600s.

5. What is another name for Woodland Indians? Why?

6. What were the jobs of women and children among historic Indians?

7. What were men's jobs?

8. How were wampum and the calumet used by the Indians?

9. Why did the Indian way of life change after Europeans came?

USING WHAT YOU HAVE LEARNED

1. What values have we learned from the Indians? What other things can we learn from them today?

2. Why do some people have incorrect ideas about Indians?

PROJECTS AND REPORTS

1. Make a drawing, model, or diorama showing life in an Indian village. You could make a model of a canoe, bark house, or wigwam. Use the models to set up an Indian village. You might add burial mounds, cooking sites, and other village activities.

2. Study and write a report on a Michigan Indian leader.

French traders bought furs from the Indians. How did they pay for these furs?

The French Explorers and Fur Traders

3

Fur Trading Was Important to Frenchmen

By the early 1800s, wealthy Europeans wanted hats and coats made of fur. Beautiful beaver furs were favorites because they lasted many years.

The fur trade brought many French *explorers* to the New World. They began to use the waterways to enter the Indian country. They explored the St. Lawrence River, Lake Huron, Lake Michigan, Lake Superior, and later the Mississippi River. Most often they used birch-bark canoes for their trips west to gather furs.

The French were unfriendly with the Iroquois Indians. To avoid them and other enemies, the French took western routes to the Upper Peninsula. At that time in history, very few people lived in the Lower Peninsula. As the French took over more and more land, they began to call the huge area New France.

The French traveled to almost all parts of the Upper Peninsula. The maps they made were quite true, even though the people did not know about the Lower Peninsula yet. They were able to find even more places to trap beavers as they canoed through the lakes and rivers.

The French were also interested in teaching Indians about

Christianity and the Bible. Many *missionaries* came to New France for this reason.

The French Explorers

The earliest French explorer was Jacques Cartier (ZHAHK kar-tee-AY). He was the first European to see the St. Lawrence River. By searching the waterways west from the St. Lawrence River, he found his way to the *territory* known as Michigan.

Another Frenchman, Samuel de Champlain (deh-sham-PLAYN) encouraged young men looking for adventure to live among the Indians and learn their language and ways. He began a settlement in Quebec, Canada, and set up many *trading posts*. Records do not show that he ever came to Michigan.

Probably the first Frenchman to step on Michigan soil was Etienne Brulé (eh-tee-EN brew-LAY). He was a young man whom Champlain had sent to live among the Indians.

Besides trapping and exploring, the French were eager to find a water route to China. They believed it was nearby. Jean Nicolet (ZHAN nih-ko-LET) lived among the Indians to learn about them. Then in 1634 he went as far as Wisconsin, looking for China. He only found more Indians.

In 1668 Father Jacques Marquette (ZHAHK mar-KET) established a *mission* at Sault Ste. Marie, which was the first settlement in Michigan.

These early French likely reached Michigan about the same time the Pilgrims landed at Plymouth in 1620. However, the French were slow to make permanent settlements. They were different from the English and Dutch pilgrims.

French Government Controlled Fur Trade

The French depended on the sale of furs for their wealth. They also depended on their strong hired traders to bring the furs. These men were the first hired workers in Michigan. They were called *voyageurs*, which means travelers. Voyageurs had to have permission from the French government to trade with Indians. These men needed canoes and

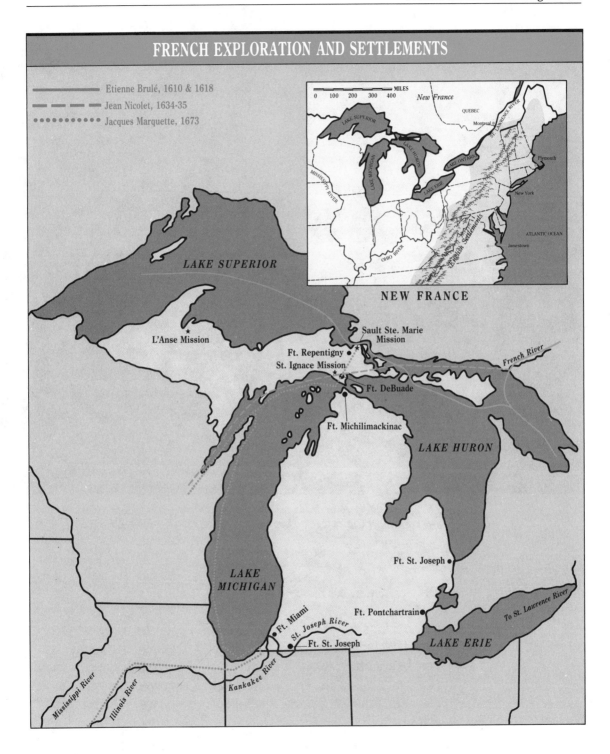

FRENCH EXPLORATION AND SETTLEMENTS

Etienne Brulé, 1610 & 1618
Jean Nicolet, 1634-35
Jacques Marquette, 1673

MILES
0   100   200   300   400

New France

QUEBEC

Montreal

ST. LAWRENCE RIVER

LAKE SUPERIOR

LAKE HURON

LAKE MICHIGAN

LAKE ONTARIO

LAKE ERIE

MISSISSIPPI RIVER

Plymouth

New York

English Settlements

OHIO RIVER

ATLANTIC OCEAN

Jamestown

NEW FRANCE

LAKE SUPERIOR

★ L'Anse Mission

Sault Ste. Marie
Mission

Ft. Repentigny
St. Ignace Mission

Ft. DeBuade

French River

Ft. Michilimackinac

LAKE HURON

LAKE
MICHIGAN

Ft. St. Joseph

Ft. Miami
St. Joseph River

Ft. Pontchartrain

To St. Lawrence River

Ft. St. Joseph

LAKE ERIE

Mississippi River

Illinois River

Kankakee River

This painting by Robert Thom shows the French arriving and setting up a cross at Sault Ste. Marie. How do you think the Native Americans felt about these newcomers?

other things for their trip, as well as goods to trade.

The Indians trapped and skinned animals such as beaver, fox, bear, otter, wolf, and muskrat. The French then *bartered* (exchanged) for the furs. The Indians received things such as blankets, knives, beads, muskets, kettles, wine, and looking glasses.

Some popular styles of beaver hats.

The D'orsay (1820)   The Continental   A clerical hat (1700s)   The Paris beau (1815)
                       cocked hat (1776)

HERE ARE SOME PRICES DURING THE VERY EARLY 1800s:

large blanket	50 muskrats
medium blanket	40 muskrats
Montreal gun	100 muskrats
beaver trap	30 muskrats
rat trap	15 muskrats
large blanket	2 beaver skins
Northwest gun	4 beaver skins
beaver trap	2 beaver skins
fathom (2 yards) of cloth	3 or 4 beaver skins
bag of flour	2 beaver skins

Today a muskrat skin costs about $10. A beaver skin can be bought for about $100. The prices change when there are greater or lesser demands for them. Why do some items from the list above cost more? Why do some things cost less?

Thousands of animals were killed for their furs. There was little thought about protecting the animals for the years ahead. As there got to be fewer and fewer animals to trap, the traders simply moved further west.

Fort Pontchartrain Built by French

In 1701 the French built Fort Pontchartrain (pon-sher-TRAIN) on the strait between Lake St. Clair and Lake Erie. This place later became the city of Detroit. *Detroit* comes from a French word which means "the straits." Antoine de la Mothe Cadillac founded the settlement at Detroit.

The French and Indian War

Very few French settlers came to New France. The fur traders did not come with their families. When war broke out between France and England in 1754, there were few people in New France to defend it against the English. The French and English wanted to control land in America. Most of the Indian nations sided with the French against the English. This is because they were getting paid by the French to trap for furs.

The Iroquois fought alongside the English. At first, the English lost many battles. When the French could no longer get men and weapons, the English won the victory. The English colonists, with the help of the Iroquois, fought hard to protect and defend their homes and farms.

In 1763 the French and Indian War ended by treaty. France signed over to England all of Canada and the French lands east of the Mississippi River, except the city of New Orleans.

The French had been friendlier with most Indians than the English had. The French did not take land from the Indians. They only wanted to trap animals for fur and to trade with the Indians. In fact, some Frenchmen had married Indian women. Even though France gave New France to England, the French tried to get the Indians to keep fighting against the English.

CHIEF PONTIAC, A BRAVE INDIAN LEADER

Pontiac was born in an Ottawa village near the Detroit River and Fort Detroit. His mother was an Ottawa and his father a Chippewa.

As he was growing up, Pontiac heard many stories about the French and the English. The French did not get along with the English. The French were friendly and traded furs with the Ottawa. The Ottawa felt, however, that the English only wanted their land. As more English families came, they forced the Ottawa to leave their land and their homes.

When war broke out between the French and the English in 1754, the Ottawa helped the French. However, the English won, and they took over Fort Detroit and land belonging to the Ottawa. There the English settled. The Ottawa had to move their homes farther away from Fort Detroit.

Now, Chief Pontiac thought, it was time to fight for their land and drive the English away. He invited other Indian nations to join in the fight against the English.

In 1763 Chief Pontiac planned to take Fort Detroit by surprise. He asked the major in charge of the fort to meet him and some of his warriors. His plan was that his men would carry guns under their blankets. Once inside the fort, they would take out

Chief Pontiac is remembered for bringing together the many Native American nations.

their guns and shoot the English. This plot, though, had been found out by the English. Chief Pontiac knew that the English were prepared for them. For this reason, he did not give the signal for his men to shoot the English. If he had, they would have all been killed.

Instead, Pontiac left the fort with his men. Even though he did not win at Detroit, Chief Pontiac was a hero to his people. He is remembered for bringing together the many Indian nations. He is also remembered as a brave leader in the fight to win back Indian land.

England was in control of the Michigan Territory from 1760 to 1796. During the Revolutionary War (1775-1781), the American colonists fought against their mother country, England. When peace was made between England and the colonies, Michigan was part of the land given to the new America.

The English were still interested in the fur trade and did not give up their trading posts until 1796. Then the United States soldiers came to the city of Monroe. There they raised the American flag for the first time on Michigan soil.

MADELINE LA FRAMBOISE, FUR TRADER

Madeline La Framboise (MAD-uh-lin luh-fram-BWAH) was a fur trader. Her father was French. Her mother was an Indian. Being raised as an Ottawa Indian, she thought of herself as an Indian and always wore Indian dresses. She was often called on to speak for Indians in trade deals. She spoke four different languages well.

LaFramboise was such a good fur trader that she and her husband built the first permanent trading post. Years later, the city of Grand Rapids was begun there.

After her husband's murder in 1806, Madeline LaFramboise kept up her work in several Michigan trading posts. The American Fur Company could not compete with her, so in 1818 they invited her to work with them.

When LaFramboise retired, she moved to Mackinac Island. There she lived for many years.

Madeline LaFramboise was a respected business woman. It was unusual for a woman to deal in the fur trade at that time. She was proud of her background. She hoped her son and daughter would become educated. She was very wise.

When she died, she was buried under the high altar in St. Anne's church on Mackinac Island.

STUDY

WORDS TO KNOW

barter	explorer	missionary	trading post
compete	mission	territory	voyageur

WHAT DID YOU LEARN?

1. Name four early French explorers.

2. Why were the French interested in the New World?

3. How did the French get furs from the Indians?

4. At the end of what war did France give up its claim to the Michigan Territory?

5. Who was Pontiac? What did he do for the French and the Indians?

6. Why was Madeline LaFramboise a good trader?

USING WHAT YOU HAVE LEARNED

1. How did Samuel de Champlain help in developing New France?

2. Why did the fur traders move even farther west than Michigan?

PROJECTS AND REPORTS

1. Pretend you are traveling with a French explorer or fur trader to the Great Lakes region. Write a diary telling about one week of your adventure. What kind of trees and animals did you see? What did you do? What did you hear? How many Indian villages did you visit? These are just a few questions that can help you write an interesting diary.

2. Prepare a list of Michigan animals. Describe the animals, tell something about their homes, food, and young. You might draw or gather pictures of the animals to display in the classroom.

3. Study and report on one French explorer, fur trader, Indian leader, or other person from this chapter.

The Great Seal of Michigan.

Michigan Becomes a State

The American Revolution

England ruled over the thirteen colonies. The English and the colonists did not get along together. For several reasons, colonists started the Revolutionary War. In 1776 they finally won their freedom from England and a treaty was signed. The United States became an *independent* country.

At that time, the Northwest Territory was claimed by both the Americans and the English. The Northwest Territory was the land between the Ohio and Mississippi rivers. The treaty said the English were to give up their trading posts in the Northwest Territory. But they didn't. This matter would later cause small battles.

Land Ordinance of 1785

In the meantime, the Land Ordinance of 1785 outlined how the Northwest Territory would be divided and sold. (An *ordinance* was a law for a territory.) The land was to be divided into square *townships* of 36 *sections*. A section is a square mile, or 640 acres. Each section would be sold at less than a dollar an acre. The money from the sale was to be used for public schools.

The Land Ordinance of 1785 divided the land into townships and sections. Try to find out from your parents which section and township you live in.

W			Base Line		
36	30	24	18	12	6
35	29	23	17	11	5
34	28	22	16	10	4
33	27	21	15	9	3
32	26	20	14	8	2
31	25	19	13	7	1

Range Line

Six Miles

A Township as Numbered
Under Ordinance of 1785

Ordinance of 1787

This law stated that the Northwest Territory would be divided into three to five territories. As soon as any one territory had 5,000 men, it could put together a government. The United States Congress, in Washington, D.C., would appoint a governor and judges.

When a territory had 60,000 people, it could write its own *constitution* and ask to become a part of the United States. But there were some rules. The people were not allowed to own slaves. There were to be public schools. People were to have certain freedoms. Some of these were the freedom to say what they wanted and attend any church they chose.

Indiana became a state in 1816 and Illinois in 1818. Then all remaining land in the Northwest Territory was called the Michigan Territory. William Hull was appointed the first governor of the Michigan Territory in 1805.

War of 1812

In 1812 a war began, and it was called the War of 1812. Several countries took part. There were two main causes for

NORTHWEST AND MICHIGAN TERRITORIES

MINNESOTA

LAKE SUPERIOR

CANADA

LAKE HURON

WISCONSIN
1848

LAKE MICHIGAN

MICHIGAN
1837

LAKE ERIE

ILLINOIS
1818

INDIANA
1816

OHIO
1803

Mississippi River

Ohio River

Michigan Territory, 1818
Northwest Territory, 1787

the war. First, American sailors were held on British ships. Great Britain was fighting a war against the French in Europe. Each side tried to keep American ships from carrying supplies and weapons to the enemy. American sailors were taken by the British and forced to work on British ships. Second, the Americans believed the British were backing the Indian uprisings in the Northwest Territory with weapons.

When the War of 1812 began, American armies withdrew from Detroit. Detroit was again under English control.

Fort Michilimackinac (mish-il-ih-MAK-uh-naw) had also fallen to the English. It was returned to the Americans in 1815.

Commander Oliver Hazard Perry fighting the English navy on Lake Erie.

U.S. Commander Oliver Hazard Perry defeated the English navy on Lake Erie. Then U.S. General William Henry Harrison defeated the English army in Canada. After that, Detroit was again in American hands.

During the Canadian battle, Chief Tecumseh was killed. He was a Shawnee chief. Chief Tecumseh wanted to keep the lands for the Indians and keep their own way of life. He was a strong leader who tried to *unite* the Indian nations and make them strong. Tecumseh's braves joined the English, hoping that together they could drive the Americans back to the eastern coast. A city in Michigan was named after Chief Tecumseh.

Chief Tecumseh was a strong leader who wanted to keep the Native American way of life. What city in Michigan is named for him?

EARLY GOVERNORS

At the head of Michigan government have been many good leaders. Here is a list of early governors of the Michigan Territory:

GOVERNOR	YEARS IN OFFICE
William Hull	1805-1813
Lewis Cass	1813-1831
George B. Porter	1831-1834
Stevens T. Mason	1834-1835

Let's read about two interesting governors.

Lewis Cass was appointed governor of Michigan in 1813. Later he was voted United States senator from Michigan. He ran for president of the United States but did not win the post.

Stevens T. Mason was appointed to take his father's place as secretary of the Michigan Territory when his father quit the job. Stevens was just nineteen years old at that time. The governor of the Michigan Territory, George B. Porter, died of cholera in 1834. Mason became the acting governor. Then he was elected to that post and was called the "Boy Governor."

What role did Lewis Cass play in Michigan? Lewis Cass High School in Detroit is named for him.

Stevens T. Mason became acting governor of Michigan when he was a young man. He has been called the "Boy Governor."

Michigan's Population Grows

Not until the state of New York completed the Erie Canal in 1825 did the *population* of Michigan Territory begin to grow. Many families were then able to come here by water.

By 1835 Michigan had more than 60,000 people. That was enough to become a new state. But Congress paid no attention to Michigan's request because of a *dispute* between Ohio and Michigan. They were fighting over a strip of land in northern Ohio. The place was Toledo, then just a small settlement.

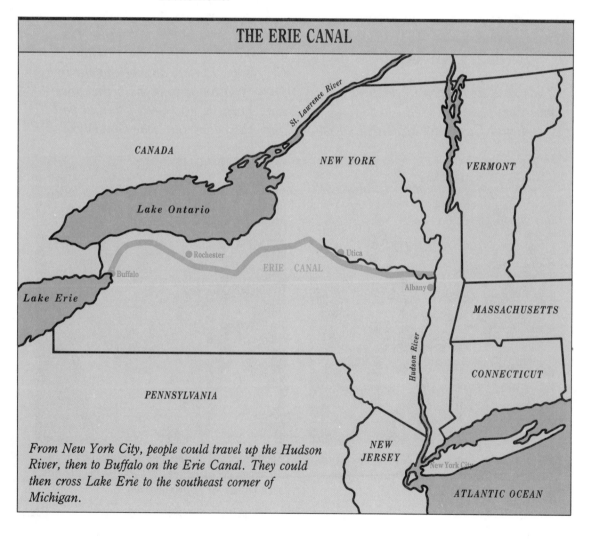

THE ERIE CANAL

From New York City, people could travel up the Hudson River, then to Buffalo on the Erie Canal. They could then cross Lake Erie to the southeast corner of Michigan.

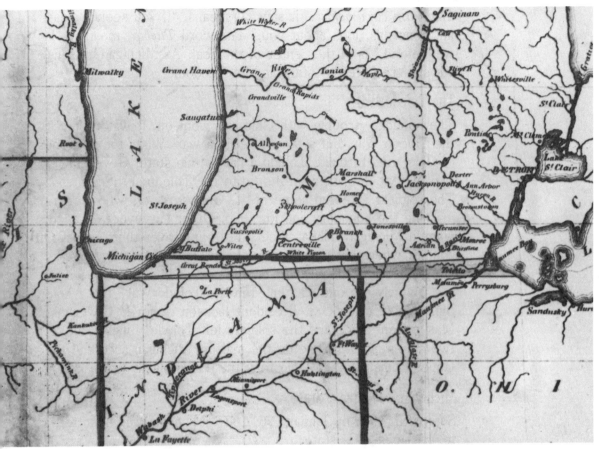

The dark wedge on this old map shows the little strip of land that caused a "war" between Ohio and Michigan.

People in Michigan went ahead anyway to prepare for statehood. A *convention* (big meeting) was called to write a constitution. The rules divided government into three parts. They also said that free white males had the right to vote. There were to be schools from the first grade through the college level. Meetings to make the laws could be attended by anyone. This constitution was voted on and passed in 1835.

The Great Seal of Michigan

At this time, the Great *Seal* of Michigan was adopted. A *motto* was written in Latin on the Great Seal. *"Si quaeris peninsulam amoenam circumspice,"* it says. It means, "If you seek a pleasant peninsula, look about you." The word *Tuebor,* meaning "I will defend," is in the center of the seal. As Michigan citizens, we still treasure our state and its freedoms.

The Toledo War

The boundary trouble with Ohio still went on. It was called the Toledo War, but it wasn't really a war. When the governor of Ohio tried to make Toledo a part of his state, Governor Mason sent the Michigan *militia* to the Toledo settlement. The soldiers arrested some of the Ohio *surveyors* who were marking the boundary line for Ohio. Other surveyors escaped when a Michigan militia officer fired a gun over their heads. Of course, when they returned safely to Ohio, they *exaggerated* stories about their escape.

Happily, no one was killed in the Toledo War. The whole thing ended when U.S. President Jackson removed Governor Mason from office and the soldiers left Toledo. Finally, the two states agreed to settle the matter. Michigan accepted the Upper Peninsula, and Ohio took the Toledo land.

Michigan Becomes a State

Soon after this, on January 26, 1837, Michigan was admitted to the Union as a state.

The people in Michigan thought that the Upper Peninsula was a poor exchange for Toledo. Very few people at that time thought Michigan got the better part of the deal. People did not know that a large amount of natural resources would be found there.

Now Michigan was made up of two peninsulas, not one as the state motto says.

The Wolverine State

Some people think that Michigan's nickname—the Wolverines—was first used by people from Ohio during the Toledo War. The wolverines were animals known to be very savage and bloodthirsty. Few of them ever lived in Michigan.

There is another story about how Michigan's nickname

Michigan's nickname comes from the wolverine.

came about. Around 1800, an inn made a specialty of serving wolf steaks. After the customer had eaten, the owner would ask, "Well, how did you enjoy your wolf steaks?" Once a customer answered, "Then, I suppose I am a wolverine?" After that, people who had eaten wolf steaks were called wolverines. Over the years, this name has been used to refer to all people living in Michigan.

Still another story about the nickname is that the Indians called settlers who took their lands wolverines. It was the worst thing the Indians could call these people. The Indians hated the wolverines.

WORDS TO KNOW

STUDY

constitution	independent	seal
convention	militia	section
dispute	motto	surveyor
exaggerate	ordinance	township
freedom	population	unite

WHAT DID YOU LEARN?

1. How did the Land Ordinance of 1785 say the Northwest Territory was to be divided?

2. Why was the Ordinance of 1787 important to Michigan?

3. What was the dispute between Ohio and Michigan about? How was it settled?

4. How many people had to live in the Michigan Territory before they could ask for statehood?

5. What Indian chief was killed during the War of 1812?

6. How old was Stevens T. Mason when he became governor?

7. What event brought more people to Michigan than ever before? Why?

8. What is the set of rules for Michigan government called?

9. When did Michigan become a state?

10. What is Michigan's motto in English?

11. What is one nickname for Michigan's people?

USING WHAT YOU HAVE LEARNED

1. Do you think our state would have been better off had it gotten Toledo rather than the Upper Peninsula? Why or why not?

2. How were the Land Ordinance of 1785 and the Ordinance of 1787 important to the Northwest Territory?

PROJECTS AND REPORTS

1. Prepare a report on Chief Tecumseh to present to the class.

2. Draw a time line to hang in the classroom. Show the major events which took place between 1812 and 1850.

3. Write a report on someone from the chapter. Here are some names to select: George Rogers Clark, Governor William Hull, Commander Oliver Hazard Perry, Governor Lewis Cass, Governor Stevens T. Mason. Why was the person a leader? What did he do for Michigan?

The State Capitol Building at Lansing.

CHAPTER

5

Michigan's Government

Rules for Everyone

We live in a world of rules and laws. They are made so that people can live together in peace and safety. There are family rules, school rules, and government rules. Can you think of other kinds of rules? Government rules are called laws.

For instance, you must attend school. This is a state law. Your parents may not park a car in front of a fire hydrant. That is a city law. If someone wants to mail a letter, there must be a stamp on the right-hand corner of the envelope. This is a *federal* law.

LISTING RULES AND LAWS

Begin making a list of all the rules and laws you obey from the time you leave school today until you return tomorrow.

Then compare lists with your classmates. Are there some rules you think are silly? Why? What might happen if they were canceled?

Why do you think people should obey the laws and rules on your list?

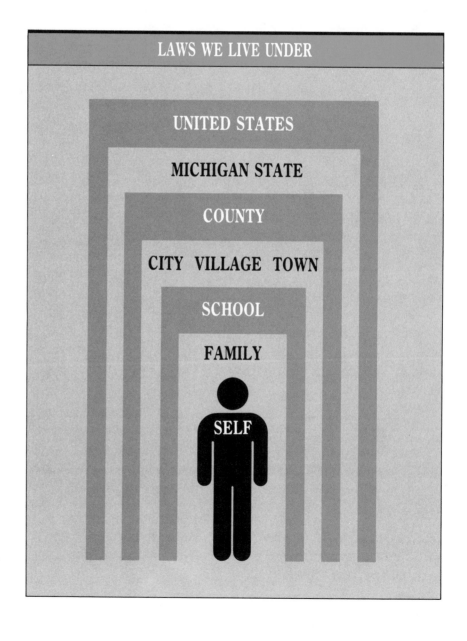

United States Constitution

About the time America became a free country, *representatives* from the thirteen colonies gathered to write the *Constitution*. This is the plan for our country's government. It tells how government is to be set up and how it is to work. It describes laws for the government and people to follow. It lists certain freedoms that people have. These are listed in the Bill of Rights, a part of the Constitution. Some of these rights are the freedom of speech and religion. Another is the freedom of the press. That means newspapers can print what they want to, as long as it is truthful.

The Constitution tells how the president and other officials are to be selected. It explains their duties and powers. It also sets up the framework for state and local governments.

In the United States, the powers of government are divided between the state and the federal governments. Each state also has its own constitution. Let's compare our state's constitution with our country's.

Michigan's Constitution

A constitutional convention was held in Detroit in 1835. There was much talk about who should have the right to vote. It ended up that every white man in Michigan over age 21 was given the right to vote.

The state constitution promised to protect, for Michigan citizens, all the rights in the U.S. Constitution. Michigan's constitution was passed in 1835.

Another constitutional convention was held in 1850. It brought about some changes. For one thing, it took away some powers of the state legislature. Men from other countries who intended to become citizens were given the right to vote. So were *"civilized"* male Indians. But black male citizens and women were not given this right.

The state constitution was changed again in 1908 and in 1963. It then was written in more detail to meet the needs of Michigan citizens. For example, Article 8 is about education. Section 9 of Article 8 is about schooling for handicapped persons.

RIGHTS FOR THE HANDICAPPED

Section 9. Institutions, programs and services for the care, treatment, education or rehabilitation of those inhabitants who are physically, mentally or otherwise seriously handicapped shall always be fostered and supported.

Who are handicapped persons? What is the government promising to do for them? Is this being done in your town?

Michigan's Government

Like the United States government, Michigan's government is divided into three branches, or parts. The *executive* branch carries out the laws. The *legislative* branch makes the laws. The *judicial* branch explains the laws.

Hundreds of people work in each branch. They are *responsible* to the state constitution and to the people of Michigan.

The Executive Branch

The governor is the head of this branch. He or she is voted into office by the citizens in Michigan.

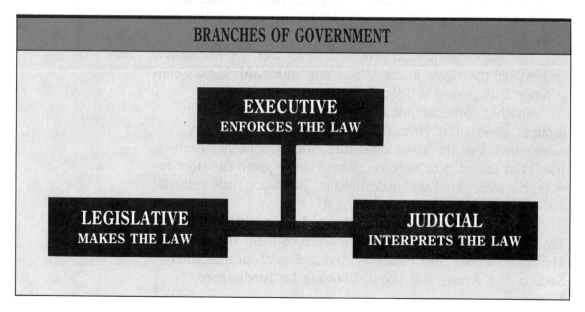

BRANCHES OF GOVERNMENT

EXECUTIVE
ENFORCES THE LAW

LEGISLATIVE
MAKES THE LAW

JUDICIAL
INTERPRETS THE LAW

*Governor John M. Engler
learned to work hard while
growing up on a cattle-
feeding farm. He also
read a lot—even daily
newspapers! In 1991
John Engler became
the governor of Michigan.*

While in office, the governor lives in Lansing. Lansing is
the state capital. When Michigan first became a state, Detroit
was the capital. Many of the state legislators were from cities
far from Detroit. Finally, they selected a new place to meet—
Lansing. Lansing is nearer the center of the state. At that
time, however, the only way to reach Lansing was by an
Indian trail. Now, many major highways connect other cities
with the capital.

When Stevens T. Mason became the state's first governor, he was just 23 years old. Now a person must be at least
30 years old to run for the office of governor. The governor
serves a four-year term and may run for office again.

The governor's duties are many. He or she sees that
laws are carried out and that there is peace and order. There
are many people to help with these duties. The director of the
State Police and the director of the Department of Conservation work with the governor.

Many other government officers also help. The secretary of state keeps records. The state treasurer takes care of the money belonging to the state. The attorney general is the lawyer for the state. Each department has hundreds of workers.

The governor is also commander-in-chief of the state militia. In case of tornadoes or other emergencies, the governor may send citizen soldiers to help keep peace and order.

Legislative Branch

The state legislature is made up of two parts. One is the Senate. The other is the House of Representatives, which is often called the House.

There are 38 members in the state Senate. They are elected to four-year terms. The House has 110 members who serve two-year terms.

The legislature makes the laws for the state. The major work of this body is done in meetings of small groups.

How Laws are Made

Let's follow one case through the system. Then study the flow chart "How a Bill Becomes Law."

One legislator felt that many lives and much money could be saved if people wore seat belts while riding in automobiles. Several studies showed that this was true.

The first task for the legislator was to write this idea in the correct form. Once written, the idea was called a *bill*. The bill was passed out to all members of the House of Representatives. There it was read aloud. Then it was assigned to a committee for study and changes. Later it was *debated* in a meeting of the whole group and was voted upon. A *majority* of members of the House favored making this bill a law. So, it was sent to the Senate. There the same steps took place, and the bill was passed. Sometimes it may take months for a bill to pass both houses.

Next it was sent to the governor. He signed it into law. Now people in Michigan must wear seat belts.

The governor could have refused to sign the bill if he did not think it would make a good law. This is called a *veto*. In

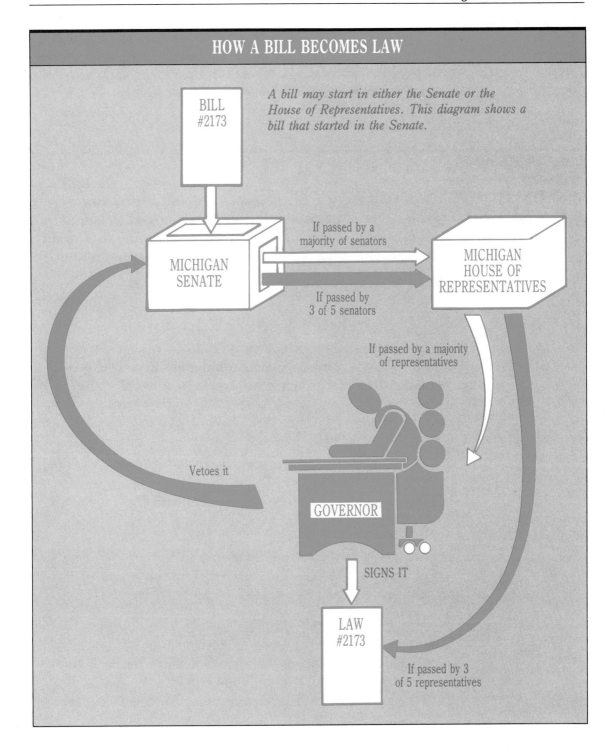

HOW A BILL BECOMES LAW

BILL
#2173

*A bill may start in either the Senate or the
House of Representatives. This diagram shows a
bill that started in the Senate.*

MICHIGAN
SENATE

If passed by a
majority of senators

If passed by
3 of 5 senators

MICHIGAN
HOUSE OF
REPRESENTATIVES

If passed by a majority
of representatives

Vetoes it

GOVERNOR

SIGNS IT

LAW
#2173

If passed by 3
of 5 representatives

such a case, the bill would be returned to the House and the Senate after 14 days. It would again need to pass both groups, but by a two-thirds majority vote. If that happened, the legislature would override the governor's veto. The bill would become law.

ACTIVITY

STATE LEGISLATURE ROLE PLAY

Act out a meeting of the state legislature in your class. Some students could be members of the Senate and others members of the House. One person should play the part of governor.

Write bills that you think would be important for your school or the state. Then see if any of the bills get passed in your legislative session.

At the end, talk about how it feels to take part in making laws. What would be hard about serving in the legislature? What part would you like best?

Judicial Branch

The judicial branch of state government helps to settle court cases that deal with state laws. There are several levels of courts. The state Supreme Court is the highest. Seven justices are elected, but they do not represent any *political party*. The supreme court handles cases that have come up through the lower courts.

A few of the lower courts are the Court of Appeals, Circuit Court, and Probate Court. The job of the courts is to decide how the laws apply to each case.

Local Government: County

There are two levels of government below the state level. One is *county government*. One job of county officers is to carry out the programs of state government. For instance, county government sells license plates for automobiles. It collects taxes for the state. County government also gives out

This is the Circuit Courtroom where court is held in Berrien County.

These students from Grand Blanc are learning how courts are run. What kinds of things do people go to court for? How can courts help us?

The Allegan County
Courthouse was
dedicated in 1889.

The Lapeer County
Courthouse is the
oldest in Michigan.
What date is shown on
the building?

food stamps to people who have signed up for that state program. The counties also run hospitals and build parks.

Besides helping the state government, counties do many services for their citizens. One office at the county building records marriages, births, and deaths. Another takes care of all county roads. Still another office gathers tax money from the citizens and later divides the money among the different branches of county government. Members elected to the county *commission* make laws for the county and decide how the county's money will be spent.

Local Government: Municipal

The other level of government below the state level is the *municipal* government. The word *municipal* has to do with city government.

In our state there are three different kinds of municipal government. Not all towns and cities have the same kind.

The mayor-council kind of city government is the oldest form. Most large cities in Michigan have this kind of govern-

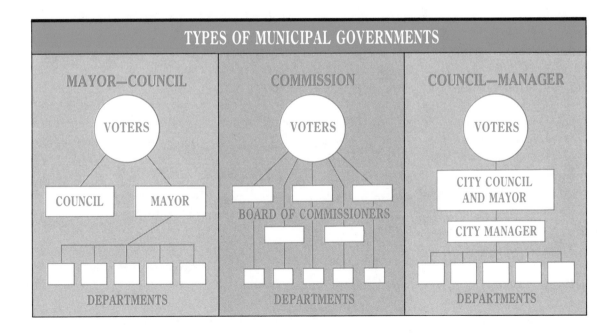

TYPES OF MUNICIPAL GOVERNMENTS

MAYOR—COUNCIL — VOTERS — COUNCIL — MAYOR — DEPARTMENTS

COMMISSION — VOTERS — BOARD OF COMMISSIONERS — DEPARTMENTS

COUNCIL—MANAGER — VOTERS — CITY COUNCIL AND MAYOR — CITY MANAGER — DEPARTMENTS

ment. The mayor is the executive leader and is voted into office. He or she is in charge of the city. It is the mayor's duty to see that *ordinances* (laws) of the city are carried out.

The city council members make the laws. The council members, too, are chosen by the people. The mayor may veto a law passed by the council, and the council may override (cancel) the mayor's veto. Citizens are invited to attend council meetings. Detroit, Dearborn, Livonia, Menominee, Niles, and Burton are a few cities which have this kind of government.

Council-manager is a second form of city government. A manager is hired by city council members to run the day-to-day business of the city. The manager is a person who has studied about cities and government. Managers prepare themselves in college for this career. Big Rapids, Port Huron, Wyoming, Benton Harbor, Saginaw, and Albion are a few cities which have this form of government.

A third kind of city government is the commission form. Citizens vote for commissioners to run the city government. These leaders make laws and head city departments such as fire, parks and recreation, and water.

The commissioners choose a mayor from among their members. The mayor is the ceremonial head of the city government. The mayor has no more power than the other commissioners. As ceremonial head, the mayor greets important visitors, attends lunches, rides in parades, and speaks at public events.

Good Citizenship Begins with You

As citizens in our town and state, we have many *privileges*. Can you name a few?

We also have *responsibilities*. With some adults, talk about what these are. We can start now to prepare for the time when we will be the grownups in our community.
Here are some ways to be a good citizen:

- Offer to help children and senior citizens to cross busy streets safely.

- Respect other people's property.

Policemen in Detroit.

- Pick up litter.

- Be a helpful friend to classmates.

- Read the newspaper to know what's going on in the world.

- Obey safety laws when riding a bicycle.

- Listen to news programs on television and radio.

Can you name other ways to be a good citizen?

As an adult, you will have even more ways to be a good citizen. Paying taxes is one way. Tax money is used to pay police officers, fire fighters, and teachers. Tax money may also be used to make and repair roads, build parks, and for other public services.

Another way to be a good citizen is to vote. This is a right that people in many countries do not have. To vote for the best choices, a person must study the *candidates* and the *issues*.

A good citizen takes an interest in the community.

IT'S THE LAW!

Sometimes a law remains on the books long after it is needed. And once in a while, a law may not be enforced. Here are some. Have you heard of these?

In Detroit it is against the law to fall asleep in the bathtub. It is also against the law to make an art work on any sidewalk space.

In Ann Arbor it is against the law to walk on any public street, alley, or park.

In Michigan it is against the law for a barbershop to be open on Sundays. It is also a law that anyone taking part in any sport on Sunday may be fined five dollars. Another law says that drinking cups must be available at public fountains. In this state it is against the law to hunt water birds by the aid or use of cattle, horses, or mules.

A 1915 law says that a person driving an automobile, upon seeing a team of horses with a driver, should stop until the horses have passed.

Why do you think these laws were made in the first place? Are they still needed today?

Political Parties

Most people who run for office at the state level are members of a political party. This is a group of people who share and agree on the same ideas about how government should be run. The job of a political party is to try to get their best people into office.

The two major political parties are the Democrats and the Republicans. There are also a few smaller parties.

The Republican party was first formed in Michigan. It began in 1854 "under the oaks," near the corner of Franklin and Second streets in downtown Jackson. So many people came to the meeting that it had to be held out-of-doors.

Elections

Elections are held to choose people for offices at all levels. Voting for all offices takes place in every community. Voting booths are set up in schools and other public buildings. Many places now use voting machines.

Sometimes a citizen cannot go to the voting booth. He or she might be handicapped or in the army or navy, or away on a trip. The person may still vote by using an *absentee ballot*. It must be marked and returned to the clerk before the day of the election.

Paying for Government Services

We expect government to run parks, libraries, museums, and do many other things for us. But these services cost money, and governments must have *revenue,* or income, to pay for them.

The Detroit Children's Museum is supported by the Detroit Board of Education.

MICHIGAN STATE REVENUE AND EXPENDITURES, 1993 ESTIMATED

STATE REVENUE FROM STATE SOURCES

$21,194 MILLIONS OF DOLLARS

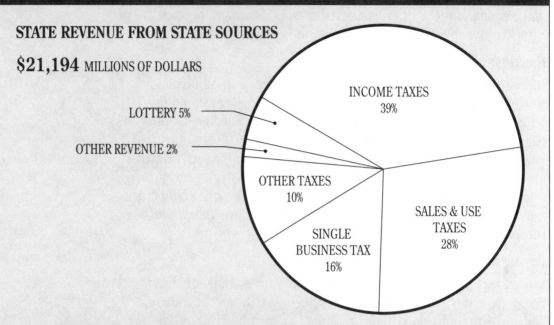

- LOTTERY 5%
- OTHER REVENUE 2%
- INCOME TAXES 39%
- OTHER TAXES 10%
- SALES & USE TAXES 28%
- SINGLE BUSINESS TAX 16%

STATE EXPENDITURES FROM STATE SOURCES

$21,191 MILLIONS OF DOLLARS

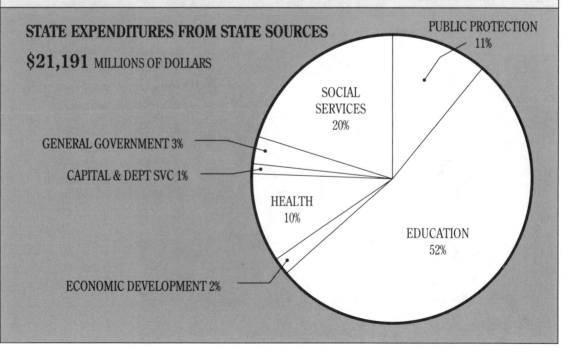

- PUBLIC PROTECTION 11%
- SOCIAL SERVICES 20%
- GENERAL GOVERNMENT 3%
- CAPITAL & DEPT SVC 1%
- HEALTH 10%
- EDUCATION 52%
- ECONOMIC DEVELOPMENT 2%

Property tax is one kind of government income. It is paid by people who own cars, houses, land, or buildings. The county gathers this tax, then sends the money to local governments. These would be townships, school districts, cities, and county offices.

Some cities have city taxes. People living or working in Detroit must pay city taxes. The amount of this tax is decided by the amount of money a person earns in a year.

The *sales tax* and the state *income tax* provide most of the money for state government. The amount of state income tax a person pays is based on one's own income.

The police and fire departments are paid for with tax monies. The health and safety departments are, too. The upkeep of roads also uses tax monies.

This photograph shows the old post office in Ann Arbor. Postal service is provided by government.

ACTIVITY

LIST OF TAXES PAID

Talk with your parent or another adult. List all the taxes your family pays. Where are the taxes paid? How often? Then make a list of services you get from paying the taxes. Write a summary statement about the importance of paying taxes.

There are also taxes on tobacco, horse racing, telephones, and other things. Other state income comes from license fees. One must pay to hunt, fish, or drive. People must buy a permit to visit a state park.

Governing the Schools in Michigan

Much of the state's income goes to run the schools. This money comes from a school tax. The state is divided into school districts. Each school district has a *board of education*.

This fifth grade class from Stanley School in Flint is celebrating an "old-fashioned" day.

The seven members of this board make the rules for the schools. They have the last word as to how the school's money will be spent.

The board of education is responsible for building and taking care of the schools. They also hire teachers and other school workers.

How much of the state's tax is used for schools? Perhaps one member of the class could call a school board member to find out.

WORDS TO KNOW

STUDY

absentee ballot
bill
board of education
candidate
civilized
commission
county government
debate
executive
federal
income tax
issue
judicial
legislative
majority
municipal
ordinance
political party
privilege
property tax
rehabilitation

representative
responsible
responsibility
revenue
sales tax
veto

WHAT DID YOU LEARN?

1. Why do people have rules and laws?
2. What is a constitution?
3. Name the three branches of government and the duties of each.
4. Where does the governor of Michigan live?
5. Who was the first governor of Michigan?
6. What are the two parts of the state legislature?
7. Explain how a bill becomes a law.
8. Name three kinds of municipal government. Explain how they are different.
9. Where does government get its income?
10. Name three things you can do to be a good citizen.
11. What can an adult do to be a good citizen?

USING WHAT YOU HAVE LEARNED

1. How is Michigan government like the United States government?

2. What kind of person should be elected as governor of Michigan?

3. What form of city government does your community have?

4. What form of city government do you think is best? Why?

PROJECTS AND REPORTS

1. Present a report to the class on any Michigan governor.

2. Make a chart of your local government. Include the names of people who hold office.

3. Invite a member of the school board to your classroom. Prepare a list of questions about his or her job.

4. Attend a meeting of your town or city council. While there, take notes: Who spoke? What was said? Who took charge of the meeting? Were other citizens in attendance? Write a page telling what you think about the meeting.

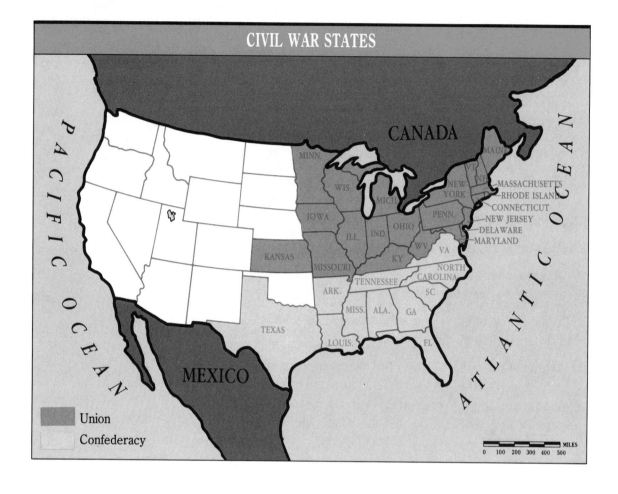

CIVIL WAR STATES

CANADA

PACIFIC OCEAN

ATLANTIC OCEAN

MEXICO

MINN.
WIS.
MICH.
IOWA
ILL.
IND.
OHIO
PENN.
NEW YORK
MAINE
MASSACHUSETTS
RHODE ISLAND
CONNECTICUT
NEW JERSEY
DELAWARE
MARYLAND
WV
VA
KY
KANSAS
MISSOURI
TENNESSEE
NORTH CAROLINA
ARK.
SC
MISS.
ALA.
GA
TEXAS
LOUIS.
FL

Union
Confederacy

MILES
0 100 200 300 400 500

Michigan and the Civil War

What Was the Civil War?

In 1861 a war started in this country. Americans in the Northern States were fighting against Americans in the Southern States. Michigan was part of the North. The fight was called the Civil War.

There were three major causes of this war. However, the issue of *slavery* is the reason most remembered. The North was against slavery. The South was in favor. Our lesson begins with some background on slave life and laws.

Slavery in the Northwest Territory

Detroit, in 1796, had about 500 people. Most wealthy Detroiters owned one slave or more. People in other Michigan settlements also owned a few slaves. Some slaves were Indian, but most were black.

The Ordinance of 1787 was a law that did not allow slavery in the Northwest Territory. However, anyone who bought slaves before 1796 was actually allowed to keep them. That year was when the Northwest Territory became part of the United States.

Anti-slavery Movement in Michigan

People who worked to end slavery were called *abolitionists*. Many church groups worked to end slavery. A Quaker, Elizabeth Margaret Chandler, began the first *anti-slavery* group in the Michigan Territory.

The argument over slaves went on for a long time. There were about half a million free blacks in the United States. Some of them, such as Sojourner Truth and Frederick Douglass, tried to get whites to fight for the freedom of all slaves. They gave speeches in many Northern states.

SOJOURNER TRUTH

Sojourner Truth was born about 1797 in New York. Her real name was Isabella Baumfree. Her parents were both slaves. When she was still a very young girl, Isabella was taken from her parents and sold. Later, after she married, her four-year-old son was taken from her and sold. She was treated this way because she was a slave.

In New York a law was passed in 1827 which gave slaves their freedom. As a free woman, Isabella Baumfree earned money by working for white families.

Then she decided to work for all black people. In 1843 she changed her name to Sojourner Truth and began her work to free all blacks. She went from place to place and spoke to many people about freedom for blacks. She continued this work until her death in 1883. Sojourner Truth was buried in Battle Creek's Oak Hill Cemetery.

Why is Sojourner Truth shown with President Abraham Lincoln?

Underground Railroad

Many people in Michigan helped slaves escape on the *"Underground Railroad."* This was not a railroad at all. It was a secret route of paths and buildings. Runaway slaves hid in the

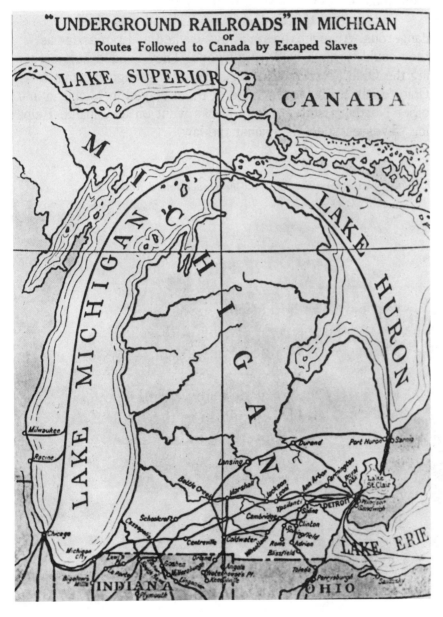

"UNDERGROUND RAILROADS" IN MICHIGAN
or
Routes Followed to Canada by Escaped Slaves

This old map shows the routes of the Underground Railroad in Michigan. Why were most of the routes located in the southeastern part of Michigan?

buildings, called *stations,* by day. People who owned the buildings and helped slaves along the way were called *conductors.* Conductors gave them food, warm clothing, and a place to sleep. One woman whose home was a station on the Underground Railroad helped 1,500 slaves. Over several years, thousands of blacks escaped to freedom.

Escaping on the Underground Railroad was always dangerous. At night the runaways walked and ran as far as they could through fields and woods. They needed help crossing the Ohio River and finding their way through Indiana or Ohio to reach Michigan. Some of them stayed in Michigan and other Northern states. Many blacks went on to Canada. Helping slaves escape was against the law.

Runaway slaves from the South on the Underground Railroad.

Blacks Living in the North

There were a large number of free blacks living in the North. They faced many problems, too. In most cities blacks lived in the poorest part of town. Their children had to go to separate schools from white children. Many blacks found it hard to get jobs since they had little education.

The Fugitive Slave Law

Mr. and Mrs. Crosswhite and their four children were escaped slaves. They had settled in a home near Marshall, Michigan. When their Kentucky owner found out where they were living, he sent a law officer to take them back to Kentucky. But the Crosswhites signaled their friends about the danger they faced. Friends helped them escape to freedom in Canada.

Kentuckians were very angry about this. They worked to get the Fugitive Slave Law passed in the U.S. Congress in 1850. This meant that runaway slaves had to be returned to their owners. But Michigan passed a law saying that U.S. marshals could not catch escaped slaves in this state. After the Fugitive Slave Law was passed, however, fewer slaves tried to run away.

HENRY BIBB, A RUNAWAY SLAVE

Henry Bibb was a runaway slave. He had had six owners. For a while he lived in Detroit. Then he went to Canada and worked for a better life for all blacks. He wrote a letter to one of his former owners.

"... But I thank God that I am not property now, but I am regarded as a man like yourself.... Think not that I have any malice [hate] against you, for the cruel treatment which you inflicted [put] on me while I was in your power....

"To be compelled to stand by and see you whip and slash my wife without mercy, when I could afford her no protection, not even by offering myself to suffer the lash in her place, was more than I felt it to be the duty of a slave husband to endure.... My infant child was frequently flogged by Mrs. Gatewood, for crying until its skin was bruised literally purple...."

From *Slave Testimony* . . . , edited by John W. Blassingame, published by Louisiana State University Press.

The Civil War

The Civil War began in 1861. The Southern States wanted to leave the Union. They felt that slaves were needed for the South's wealth. Blacks worked in the cotton fields on large *plantations*. Michigan and other Northern states wanted free farmers and workers to settle on the land. They did not think one person had a right to own another person. So the country was divided over this question. The North was against the South.

When Abraham Lincoln became president, some of the Southern states *seceded* (withdrew) from the Union. Soon other states followed them, until the country was divided.

Michigan Supports President Lincoln

President Abraham Lincoln asked for soldiers from every state to help fight in the war. Austin Blair was governor of Michigan at the time. He sent about 1,000 men to Washington, D.C., shortly after the beginning of the war. The war lasted about 4½ years. During that time, Michigan sent soldiers, weapons, clothes, and food to the Northern army. Most people in Michigan favored the cause of the North.

The *volunteers* for the army were trained at Fort Wayne before they left for Washington, D.C. Soldiers came from Detroit, Kalamazoo, Niles, and other cities. More than 90,000 Michigan men of all races and different backgrounds served in the Union army.

A Soldier's Life

Life as a soldier was difficult. The men had to work long hours, drilling and marching. Often, they did not have enough to eat. They did not have enough warm clothing. Many soldiers became sick. Some wanted to go home. A few *deserted* the army but were caught and punished.

One well-known soldier was George A. Custer from Monroe, Michigan. He was a brave leader who led soldiers in many Civil War battles. (Later he was killed by the Sioux Indians in the Battle of Little Big Horn in 1876.)

MICHIGAN ARMY REFUSES TO TAKE GEORGE HARRIS, A BLACK

George Harris lived in Michigan and wanted to be a soldier. He was not allowed to join the army because he was black. He left Michigan and joined a black army group in another state. George Harris later took part in the battle which helped to win the city of Charleston, South Carolina, for the Northern army. This was a very important battle during the Civil War.

Later blacks from Michigan did serve in the army.

How would you describe the general feeling toward blacks during the Civil War in Michigan?

Headquarters of the First Ambulance Corps during the Civil War.

Posters like this one urged men to enlist in the infantry to fight in the Civil War.

After the War

The Civil War ended in 1865. The South *surrendered* to the North. This meant that freedom for slaves had been won. Most of the soldiers and nurses quickly returned to their homes, farms, and jobs. A few remained in the army.

Summary

When the Civil War ended, a plan was made so the Southern

This sketch of General George A. Custer shows his bravery in battle.

states could come back into the Union. The United States would again become one country.

The Civil War made life better for people in many ways. The North (this included Michigan) was stronger and wealthier than ever before. More factories were built to make clothing and weapons for the army. Farmers were busy growing food for the soldiers and for other people. More people came to Michigan to work in the factories and on the farms. Some people came from other states.

New railroads were built, connecting the East with the Far West. Roads were improved for wagons.

After the war, blacks still had a hard life. Getting their freedom was not enough. They needed jobs. They were free but without land, without education, and without money.

An important *amendment* (change) was added to the United States Constitution. The Fifteenth Amendment was accepted by the Michigan legislature in 1869. It gave all men the right to vote. Women did not win that right until 1920.

STUDY

WORDS TO KNOW

abolitionist

amendment

anti-slavery

conductor

desert (verb)

native-born

pension

plantation

secede

slavery

station

surrender

Underground Railroad

volunteer

WHAT DID YOU LEARN?

1. What was the major issue of the Civil War?

2. What law did not allow slaves in the Northwest Territory?

3. What were people who worked to end slavery called?

4. How did the Underground Railroad help escaped slaves?

5. What law said that runaway slaves had to be returned to their masters?

6. In what year did the Civil War begin? When did it end?

7. Who was the president of the United States during the Civil War?

8. What was life like in Michigan during the Civil War?

9. What right did the Fifteenth Amendment to the Constitution deal with?

USING WHAT YOU HAVE LEARNED

1. Why did blacks want their freedom?

2. What was life like for blacks in Michigan after the war?

PROJECTS AND REPORTS

1. Interview someone who serves in the armed forces to learn about that career. What kind of work do they do? How are they treated? Report to the class.

2. Write a report about Sojourner Truth, Frederick Douglass, or any other abolitionist.

*West of Oscoda stands the Lumberman's Memorial. It is dedicated to the
lumbermen who made Michigan a leading lumbering state.*

Lumbering, a Key to Michigan's Growth

Lumbering Brought Jobs

Lumbering became an important way to make a living in Michigan from the 1850s to the 1900s. It also caused growth in other kinds of work. Sawmills were needed. So were railroads, ships, and furniture factories. As people came to work in those businesses, they needed homes, food, clothing, and equipment. These needs made jobs for many other people.

Maple sap is collected in buckets, then boiled down to make maple syrup.

Trees: A Valuable Resource

Can you imagine a view of Michigan in 1800? All the land, except for 35,000 acres in Kalamazoo, Calhoun, Cass, and St. Joseph counties, was covered with trees. Today there are still many trees in the Upper Peninsula.

Seventy-nine different kinds of trees are native to Michigan. Sixteen other kinds have been brought here. Some trees are found statewide. Others grow only in the north or the south of the state.

TREES FOUND STATEWIDE

aspen	sugar maple
basswood	tamarack
blue dogwood	white cedar
cottonwood	white pine

FOUND MOSTLY IN NORTHERN MICHIGAN

aspen	jack pine
balsam fir	mountain ash
hemlock	striped maple

FOUND MOSTLY IN SOUTHERN MICHIGAN

American crab	sassafras
chestnut	silver maple
hickory	sycamore
oak	tulip tree
red bud	walnut

Thousands and thousands of acres of white pine grew in Michigan forests in the early 1800s. These trees were in great demand because their soft wood was easy to work with. *Timber* (what harvested trees are called) was needed to make houses, furniture, and covered wagons. Handles for hammers, hoes, railroad ties, ships and boats, and many other things were also made of wood. Scrap lumber was even burned in fireplaces for heat in winter. Scrap wood was also used as fuel

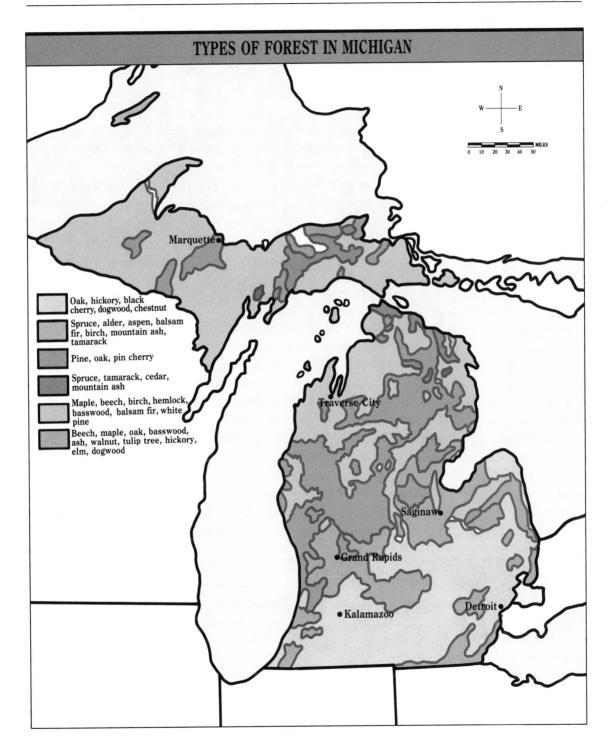

TYPES OF FOREST IN MICHIGAN

Oak, hickory, black cherry, dogwood, chestnut

Spruce, alder, aspen, balsam fir, birch, mountain ash, tamarack

Pine, oak, pin cherry

Spruce, tamarack, cedar, mountain ash

Maple, beech, birch, hemlock, basswood, balsam fir, white pine

Beech, maple, oak, basswood, ash, walnut, tulip tree, hickory, elm, dogwood

Marquette

Traverse City

Saginaw

Grand Rapids

Kalamazoo

Detroit

"When Pine Was King" is the title of this painting by Robert Thom. Early loggers cut many of the white pine trees in the state. In 1955, the white pine became the Michigan state tree.

to heat the *brine* in harvesting salt. The salt business became very important.

Michigan's rivers and lakes were important to the lumber business. Logs could be floated from the forests to the sawmills. This was easier and cheaper than hauling them overland by horse and wagon.

The white pine was chosen as the state symbol for Michigan. Today few white pine trees grow here. Some very tall ones may be seen at the Hartwick State Park near Grayling. There, white pines grow in their natural *environment*.

TREES I KNOW

ACTIVITY

Make a list of all the kinds of trees which grow on the street where you live. Find out which kinds are native to Michigan and which have been brought to this state.

Draw a picture of your favorite tree. Write a paragraph telling what you like best about the tree.

The log drive down the Muskegon River. Why were rivers an important way to transport logs?

Early Uses of Trees

When the French and English came to Michigan, they cut down trees to build homes, forts, and missions. The French even built windmills to make water power for sawing the logs.

Later the English used huge oak logs for building ships. After the War of 1812, Americans cut these *hardwood* trees. They built ships for use on the Great Lakes.

Lumbering in the Saginaw Valley

The Saginaw Valley was the first place in Michigan to sell lumber. There were plenty of white pine trees in the forests. *Lumberjacks* would cut down the trees near the rivers and float the logs to the sawmills. Then the lumber would be shipped to the mouth of the Saginaw River. From there it was sent by ships to other states, using the New York and Ohio canals. Later the railroads carried the lumber. They were cheap and fast.

This was the world's champion load of logs at the A. J. Scott Camp at Hope Creek, Iosco County, in 1888.

The Sidney O'Neff *is one of the many ships which transported logs along rivers and canals.*

Lumberjacks came from Maine, Canada, and the Scandinavian countries to work in Michigan. They brought their tools with them and showed new workers how to cut trees fast and safely.

Henry H. Crapo, who later became a governor, first came to Michigan to make money in the lumber business.

The town of Saginaw began to grow and get wealthy. Before, it had been a French fur-trading post. From Saginaw, lumbering spread west and north in Michigan. By 1900 many lumberjacks were leaving Michigan. They were heading for the forests in the northwestern United States and Canada.

Cutting the Trees

It was best to cut the trees during the winter. The logs could be pulled on *bobsleds* to the rivers. Along the rivers, the logs were piled 20 to 30 feet high. Each log was marked on both ends with the initial or sign of its owner.

Logging trains on skis were used in the winter time.

Log marks were used
to identify the logs
belonging to different
lumbering companies.

When the ice melted in the spring, rivermen began to push the logs downstream. This was a hard and dangerous job. The rivermen, with their heavy spiked boots, worked night and day until the drive was over. Running the logs downstream was called *booming*. The men who did that job were the toughest and strongest in the business.

At the sawmills, the logs were sorted and stored until needed.

New Ideas to Make Lumbering Easier

Saws, tools, and other machines were improved by Michigan lumberjacks as they worked in the camps. This made their jobs easier and safer.

Winfield Scott Gerrish was one such *inventor*. He used a locomotive to pull flatcars loaded with logs from the woods to the rivers. This meant loggers could move farther into the forests. It was now possible to cut more trees and to work year round. Moving lumber from one place to another was very important for good business.

Another *invention* was the "big wheel." It was developed by Silas Overpack. These wheels were eleven feet or so across. They made it possible for a team of horses to carry three or four logs at a time.

The first sawmills were built in the Upper Peninsula in 1822. The logging *industry* began to boom in the 1800s. Today almost all of Michigan's lumber comes from the Upper Peninsula.

Life in the Lumbering Camps

The men who cut logs lived in lumbering camps. They slept and ate there. The lumberjacks worked long hours. Only strong, hard workers could do the job.

Lumberjacks were often Irishmen, Swedes, Finns, or Norwegians. They were also French-Canadians or Americans from Maine. Some lumberjacks were farmers from southern Michigan. They would spend the winter in the camps earning money. Then they would return home for the spring and summer farm work.

"Big Wheels" made hauling logs easier.

In their camps the men would sing and tell stories. They told stories about legendary lumberjacks such as Silver Jack, Joe Fournier, and Seney. They enjoyed very much the tall tales about Paul Bunyan.

The stories say that Paul Bunyan was a giant of a lumberjack who had a huge blue ox. He was the strongest and biggest lumberjack in the world.

PAUL BUNYAN TALE

"One time when Paul was logging in these parts—on Lake Superior, I recall it was—he lost his pet mosquito, Annabelle. He'd taught her not to bite him, but to sit atop his hat and warn her relatives to keep their distance. Annabelle was quite a girl.

"Well, one day Paul was trying to cut a pine—two hundred feet from butt to tip it was—in just three strokes. He did it, too. But when the pine crashed down, it brushed against his hat. And Annabelle? When he took off his hat to look for her, she wasn't anywhere to be seen. 'She jumped,' Paul groaned. 'She probably got scared. I'll find her if it takes a hundred years.'

" . . . .'I'll find her if it takes a hundred years,' Paul Bunyan said, and started out to look. He took a couple of strides straight south, and when he couldn't spot a trace of Annabelle, he dropped a tear. The tear became a lake—Brule Lake!

"He dropped another tear, and splash! the lake began to overflow its banks and make a river flowing south and east. And that's our river, still going strong.

"Then Paul reached out and grabbed an old dead tree to comb the countryside for Annabelle. The twigs scratched out along the earth, and made a channel for Paul Bunyan's tears. Each tear became a stream—the Iron, the Paint, the Nett, the Michigamme, Sturgeon, and the like.

"The tree's main stream scratched out a wider furrow—the Menominee—and pulled the smaller streams to it.

"But still no Annabelle! Paul trudged along and said, 'I'll dig for her. She must have jumped into a hole somewhere.' He took a spade and dug a trench—Green Bay! And dug and dug until he had a lake. Lake Michigan!

"The dirt he threw out toward the setting sun became the Rocky Mountains, pile on pile. The dirt he shoveled to the other side became the Appalachians, for a fact. But still no Annabelle! He lost his mitt—full of earth the mitt was, with all his diggin'. It became the lower part of Michigan. You can see the shape of it to this day.

"Still he hadn't found his Annabelle. Who knows what might have happened next to change the shape of this old continent . . . .

"Who knows what might have happened? But, just then, Paul heard a sound somewhere near his ear. He put his hand into his shock of hair and . . . pulled out Annabelle!

"She said she had got chilly on his hat and crawled inside the blanket of his hair when he first started chopping down that pine. She had fallen asleep . . . and just woke up in time to see a spade of dirt hiding the sun. If Paul put out the sun, Annabelle complained, he was going to make her colder than ever.

"And so Paul Bunyan threw his spade into Lake Michigan. It made an island up at Mackinac.

"Then he and Annabelle went back to camp to cut more pines. And if you don't believe the story's true, just take a little walk along the Brule or the Menominee some day in spring. And you will find, I bet, that Annabelle has warned her relatives to keep their distance from Paul Bunyan's hat. They've settled down to wait for us instead. If you're in doubt, just take a walk and see!"

Aileen Fisher
From *Timber! Logging in Michigan!*

Paul Bunyan and Babe.

Making Furniture in Michigan

A cabinetmaker, William Haldane, settled in Grand Rapids about 1835. He was one of the first makers of furniture. He used hardwoods to make his tables and cabinets. There were plenty of hardwood trees in Michigan. Some of Haldane's furniture is on display in the Grand Rapids Public Museum.

Loss of Forests

There was much waste in the forests. Sometimes more trees were *felled* than were needed. They were left to rot.

Fires killed thousands of trees. In 1881 a fire burned many acres of forest land in the Thumb area. St. Clair, Lapeer, Tuscola, Huron, and Sanilac counties were most

A classic chair design made by William Haldane.

A furniture maker is reproducing the design from an antique chair. This photograph was taken at Baker Furniture Inc. in Holland in the 1950s.

The airplane became a faster way of getting goods to markets.

affected. Many lives were lost. People were left homeless. Clara Barton, director of the Red Cross, gave help to these people. This was the first time the Red Cross was there to help people in need. Barton had just organized the Red Cross a few weeks before the Michigan fire.

Lumbering in Michigan Today

Still, there are many people who work in lumbering. Some workers cut trees and replant the forests. Christmas trees and paper making are important businesses. About 700 farmers grow Christmas trees on 40,000 acres of Michigan land. Millions of trees are shipped to other states, some even to Hawaii. Our state produces 95% of the world's supply of bird's-eye maple. This is a very fine wood used in furniture. When polished, it has many marks that look like birds' eyes. The making of wood pulp for paper goods has also grown.

The forests are also important for recreation and beauty. Michiganians and visitors from other states and countries enjoy camping and walking in the forests.

Conservation in Michigan

In the early years, there was no interest in *conserving* or replanting forests. It appeared that the supply of trees would

This land has been misused by lumbering companies. How have lumbering practices changed? Why is this kind of land use no longer possible?

These workers are caring for young pine seedlings which will be used by lumbering companies to reforest the areas which they have logged.

never end. Then people began to see that they were using the forests faster than new trees were growing.

Much work has been done to prevent and control forest fires. Millions of seedlings have been planted by the state and lumber companies to bring new crops of trees. Forests are an important natural resource for years ahead.

STUDY

WORDS TO KNOW

bobsled	industry
booming	invention
brine	inventor
conserve	lumbering
fell	lumberjack
hardwood	timber

WHAT DID YOU LEARN?

1. How much of Michigan's land was covered with trees in 1800?

2. Which trees were most plentiful in Michigan?

3. Who worked in the lumbering industry?

4. Describe the inventions which made lumbering more easy and safe.

5. How were the logs taken to market?

USING WHAT YOU HAVE LEARNED

1. Why was Paul Bunyan a famous legend?

2. Why is Michigan no longer a frontier state?

3. Why should we protect our natural resources? How should we protect them?

PROJECTS AND REPORTS

1. Make a list of fifteen kinds of trees which grow in Michigan. Tell which ones are native and which ones are not.

2. Draw pictures of five kinds of trees and their leaves. Tell where the trees may be found. On an outline map of the state, mark the places where they may be growing.

3. Write a tall tale using Michigan animals and trees. Why do people enjoy listening to tall tales? Collect everyone's stories and publish them in a class book.

4. Find out what can be done to prevent forest fires. What causes forest fires? What kind of damage is caused by forest fires?

5. Find tales about Paul Bunyan. Share your favorite tale with your classmates. You might wish to draw a picture to go with your story.

Mining copper was hard work. Look at the jobs each of these men is doing.
Which job would you rather do? Why?

Mining

Ghost Towns in Michigan

Did you know that Michigan perhaps has more *ghost towns* than states such as Nevada and Wyoming? Some towns that once were busy places are now empty. All the people have moved away. That is why they are called ghost towns. Most of these are old mining towns and sawmill towns. Some have railroad tracks nearby.

When other states began to produce copper from ore more cheaply than Michigan could, mines in Michigan were closed. People left their homes and went to other states to find jobs. And when the supply of white pine trees ran out, lumber workers moved west for jobs.

There are hints that will help us know if a place we see today is a ghost town. You might see straight rows of trees among overgrown bushes and weeds. This would be a hint that people might have planted the trees along a street. Lilacs, roses, or other flowers which do not grow wild give us a hint that someone lived there. Deep ruts in the dirt roads might mean that wagons used to pass by. Pieces of sidewalk and forgotten cemeteries could be helpful clues.

Marlborough in Lake County is a ghost town. Several hundred people went to live there in 1901 and worked for the

Great Northern Portland Cement Company. They used the *marl* found there. It was a mixed soil of clay, sand, and limestone. Because business was poor, the factory closed in 1908. Today remains of the factory can be seen, but no people.

Mineral Resources

People mine minerals which are often found underground. Some of these are copper, iron ore, coal, limestone, and salt.

Mining is the *process* of getting the minerals from under the ground. This work is hard and dangerous. It takes great skill. From some of these minerals, people make buildings, machines, and tools. From certain others, power, heat, and light can be made. Our way of life is much better because of minerals.

These men are pouring copper ingots or bars. Why are they doing this? This photograph was taken in 1910.

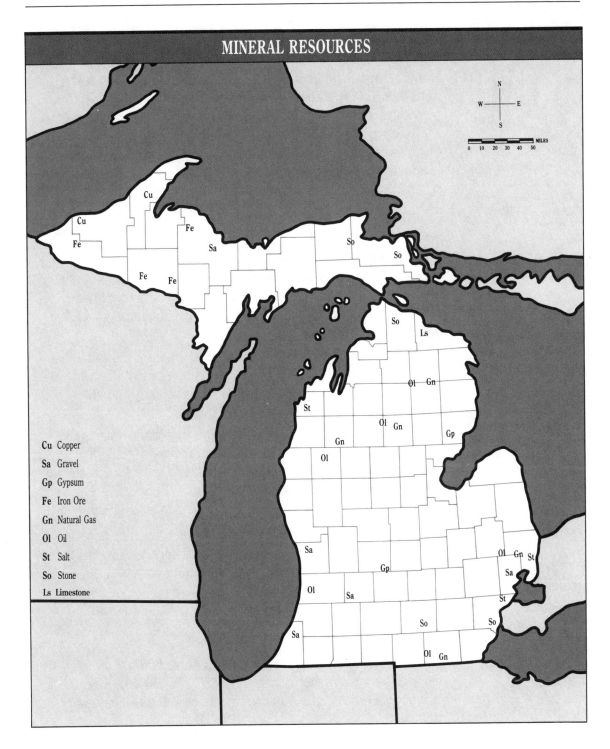

MINERAL RESOURCES

Cu Copper
Sa Gravel
Gp Gypsum
Fe Iron Ore
Gn Natural Gas
Ol Oil
St Salt
So Stone
Ls Limestone

WHO USES MINERALS?

ACTIVITY

Look around at objects in the classroom such as desks, chairs, doors, etc. Were any minerals or forest products used to make these objects? Which ones? Make two lists on the chalkboard to show which objects were made from minerals and which were made from trees.

Copper is Discovered

Early Michigan Indians found copper in *boulders,* or large rocks. The Indians had made lovely copper ornaments and necklaces. They also made weapons and tools from the copper. It is believed that early Michigan Indians worked at least 10,000 copper *pits* on Isle Royale.

Later, the French found copper. But they did not mine it. The English, in 1771, began mining copper near the Ontonagon River. They were not able to make money, so they stopped mining.

Governor Lewis Cass planned an *expedition* to explore Michigan in 1820. Henry R. Schoolcraft was a geologist on the trip. He described what he saw in 1821. He reported seeing plenty of mineral resources in the Upper Peninsula. The group had seen the Ontonagon boulder which had pure copper in it.

Reports about the Ontonagon boulder excited people's interest in Michigan. People soon came here looking for adventure. They also hoped to make money.

Houghton—Mining Capital

Douglass Houghton was a Detroit doctor. He was chosen state geologist by Governor Mason in 1837. In 1842 he became the mayor of Detroit. He also taught classes at the University of Michigan.

ONTONAGON BOULDER

The Ontonagon boulder was a huge one, at least 6,000 pounds. A Detroiter by the name of Julius Eldred wanted to make money by showing the boulder in Detroit. It was a big job to get it there. People in Detroit had to pay 25 cents to see it.

It is believed that Eldred paid a Chippewa Indian $150 for the big rock. Eldred had a permit from the government to remove the boulder. Then the government thought it best to keep the boulder in Washington, D.C. Today it may be seen in the National Museum of Natural History.

This sketch shows the discovery of the amazing Ontonagon Boulder. This 6,000-pound boulder is now at the National Museum of Natural History in Washington, D.C.

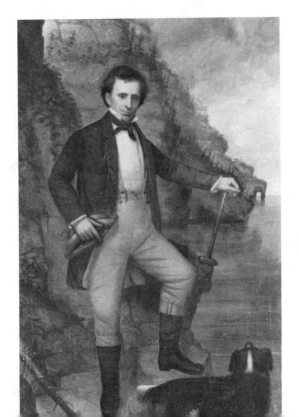

Douglass Houghton was a doctor, geologist, teacher, and politician. The town of Houghton was named for him.

In 1843 there was a great rush for jobs in the mines. The town of Houghton, named after Michigan's first geologist, became America's first "mining capital." Between 1847 and 1887, Michigan was the leading producer of copper in the United States.

During the early 1850s copper was sold to the U.S. government. It was used for buttons, canteens, and cannons.

Miners

There was a great need for miners in Michigan. Many men came here from Cornwall, England, when mines there closed. They settled in the Keweenaw Peninsula. It was one of the

Mining companies in the Upper Peninsula employed many immigrants.

richest areas for copper. These men were skilled miners. They became the captains, foremen, and managers in the mines. The Cornish miners taught the Irish, Swedes, and Norwegians how to work in the mines. They also taught the Finns, Italians, Austrians, Hungarians, and others who came to work in the mines.

The copper-bearing rocks near Houghton are believed to be among the oldest rocks in the world.

When copper became cheaper in other states, Michigan's mines closed. Today very little copper is mined here.

Iron Ore

Iron ore was discovered near the city of Negaunee by William A. Burt in 1844. He was a surveyor for the government. One day he noticed the needle of his *magnetic compass* shaking strangely. He figured out that this was caused by the iron ore *deposits* nearby.

Burt was a clever man. He invented the *solar compass*. He made the first writing machine (typewriter). He built many sawmills. He wrote important reports on the geology of Michigan. These are still used today.

One of the first leaders in iron mining was John Wood. He became known as "Iron." This nickname, added to his own name of Wood, gave the city of Ironwood its name.

Most iron mines were near Lake Superior and Lake Michigan. The lakes were used to ship the ore to factories quickly and cheaply. Marquette and Escanaba are still important iron ore shipping centers.

The three richest iron areas in Michigan were Marquette, Menominee, and Gogebic. The best iron ore has already been mined. What is left cannot be mined easily and cheaply now. Perhaps someday there may be new ways to mine ore.

Soo Locks

To help the iron industry, the state government built a canal around the St. Mary's Rapids. This swift place on the river kept ships from going between Lake Superior and the lower lakes. Lake Superior is 22 feet higher than the other Great Lakes.

Charles T. Harvey was in charge of building the canal and *locks*. It was a hard job, but he finished on time, in 1855.

The Soo Locks are still in use today. The canal was just over a mile long and 100 feet wide. Two huge locks lay side by side. Each was 350 feet long and 70 feet wide. Gates were used to raise water to the height of Lake Superior. Then ships were lowered to the level of Lake Huron. More locks have been added since then.

Today the Soo is one of the busiest canals in the world. This waterway helped Michigan become a great *manufacturing* state.

This is the Weitzel Lock at Sault Ste. Marie. Locks made it possible for ships to travel between lakes.

St. Lawrence Seaway

The St. Lawrence Seaway was finished in 1959. It gave Michigan a waterway to the oceans. Foreign ships can now dock at any of the Michigan *ports*.

Salt Mining

About the time of the Civil War, large amounts of salt were discovered in Michigan.

By the 1800s Michigan made about half of the country's salt. In 1891 J. B. Ford drilled a salt well in Wyandotte. Salt brine was brought up to the surface and the water was evaporated. Salt crystals that remained were then shoveled into barrels and sent to market.

Limestone is one product mined in Michigan. Limestone quarried near Rogers City is loaded onto freighters at the nearby port of Calcite.

Michigan is the country's leader in *saline* products. These are made by processing the salt. Twenty-nine percent of all the country's salt deposits are found in our state.

Salt has many uses. At Midland, H. H. Dow found a way of making a metal called *magnesium* from salt. The Dow Chemical Company makes chlorine from salt. Chlorine is used in *chemicals,* drugs, and dyes.

Many other things are made from salt. Soda is one. Soda ash is used in the manufacture of plate glass for windows. Baking soda and soaps are also processed from salt.

Mineral Uses Today

As more people came to Michigan, there was a need for building materials. Bricks were made from clay and powdered *shale.* Cement was made by heating powdered shale and limestone together.

Gypsum is used to make wall plaster, chalk, pottery, and other things. Coal was mined in Williamston during the mid-1970s.

While some kinds of mines have closed, many remain open. A few of the mines have been opened for visitors to see. A few ghost towns are being changed into resort towns.

Michigan's minerals meant jobs for many people. Factories of all kinds were built to process these resources. Automobiles, machinery, engines, and boats needed minerals. So did many other things which we use every day.

FAYETTE, GHOST TOWN FOR VISITORS

Fayette is a ghost town in the Upper Peninsula. When the Jackson Iron Company shut down their business in 1891, all the people moved out of Fayette. The buildings have been saved and people can visit there.

A self-guided walk around town leads to a museum, old buildings, and beautiful views of the cliffs and Lake Michigan.

When the furnaces of the Jackson Iron Co. were running, Fayette was a busy place. When the furnaces closed in 1891, it became a ghost town.

STUDY

WORDS TO KNOW

boulder
cemetery
chemical
deposit
expedition
ghost town
lock
magnetic compass

manufacturing
marl
pit
port
process
saline
shale
solar compass

WHAT DID YOU LEARN?

1. What is a ghost town?

2. Why does Michigan have ghost towns?

3. Name one ghost town. What was its chief business?

4. What is mining?

5. Who first discovered copper in Michigan?

6. What big rock excited people's interest in Michigan?

7. Where was America's first mining capital?

8. Who was the first to discover iron ore in Michigan?

9. Why isn't much iron being mined here now?

10. How was the problem of St. Mary's Rapids solved?

11. Name four saline products.

12. What is happening to some ghost towns today?

USING WHAT YOU HAVE LEARNED

1. What are mineral resources?

2. How might more jobs be created for people in the Upper Peninsula?

3. Why were the Soo Locks and the St. Lawrence Seaway important in the development of our mineral resources?

4. Why are mineral resources important?

PROJECTS AND REPORTS

1. Make a report on any person mentioned in this chapter or anyone else who worked with Michigan's mineral resources.

2. Make a map of the state. Point out where the mineral resources can be found. Also, point out the shipping routes, the Soo Locks, and the St. Lawrence Seaway.

3. Make drawings or models of the Soo Locks. Prepare to show them to your classmates.

5. Make a science experiment to show how salty water can be evaporated to leave salt crystals.

6. Find the names of ghost towns in our state. Then find them on a map. Where were most of them found? Why?

7. Study about any mineral mined in our state today. Make a poster to show the class how it is used.

Fishing is a favorite sport in Michigan.

CHAPTER

Fishing

Water Everywhere

S tand anywhere in Michigan. You are not more than five miles from a lake or a stream. And you will never be more than 85 miles from one of the Great Lakes. Michigan has much water. The waters are filled with many fish.

Fish had been a part of the *diet* for the Indians and for the early explorers. The early Indians fished from their canoes in the Great Lakes and rivers of Michigan. Fish was plentiful.

A Chippewa village by the rapids at Sault Ste. Marie in 1850. How did these people make a living?

Fishing for a Living

Fishing became an important way to make a living by the 1860s. Whitefish, lake trout, and perch were caught and sold. *Refrigeration* was a big help to fish companies. Before refrigerators, there was no good way to keep the fish cold. They had to be cleaned, packed in salt, and then shipped to markets in barrels. The fish were smoked or salted to keep them from spoiling.

Commercial fishing was a good business during the late 1800s. Fishing villages such as Bay Port and Saugatuck were founded on the shores of Michigan's lakes. In Mackinac County there were over 30 fishing companies. In 1873 the Fish Commission was set up. Members of this group tried to increase the amount of lake trout and whitefish in the Great Lakes. *Hatcheries* (places for hatching fish eggs) were built. Small fish were *planted* in the lakes and rivers. All these measures were taken to help the fish industry.

People in the fishing industry liked these services. But they did not obey some laws. They caught the largest possible number of fish without care for the future.

Killer fish like the sea lamprey destroyed millions of fish in the Great Lakes and hurt the fishing industry.

The fishing industry did poorly in the 1900s. Chemicals and wastes from fish factories and other factories were dumped into the rivers. The *pollution* destroyed thousands of fish and made other fish dangerous to eat.

Sea lampreys entered the Great Lakes through the St. Lawrence Seaway and killed millions of fish. The lampreys would attack the fish and suck out their blood. It has been possible to control the lampreys by using chemicals and electric screens at their *spawning grounds*. The alewives, a small North American fish, also destroyed many fish.

Commercial fishing is no longer a big industry in Michigan. But some commercial fishing is still done today.

Fishing for Fun

Trout and other fish have been planted in the lakes and rivers. The coho salmon were planted in Michigan waters in the 1960s. They were selected to control the alewives. They are also popular game fish.

These are some of the popular game fish found in Michigan waters. Have you ever gone fishing and caught any of these kinds of fish?

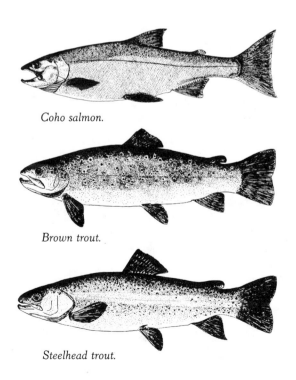

Coho salmon.

Brown trout.

Steelhead trout.

Chinook salmon.

Lake trout.

There are plenty of whitefish, herring, perch, and pickerel in Michigan waters. Fishing is allowed only during certain times and seasons. A state *license* is needed before a person can go fishing.

WHO'S BEEN FISHING?

ACTIVITY

Take a count of students who have ever gone fishing. Talk about what each person liked best about fishing. What didn't they like? Where did they go? Find the spot on a map.

Discuss why fish is good to eat. What does it add to our diet?

Ice fishing is a fun winter sport. It began in Michigan when some fishermen caught bluegills through a hole in the ice.

Department of Natural Resources

Through the work of the Department of Natural Resources, more and more fish are to be found in Michigan's lakes and rivers. A little over 800,000 coho salmon were planted in

Fish are being transferred from fish hatchery tanks to Michigan streams. Hatcheries are very important to Michigan fishermen. Without hatcheries, what would probably happen to Michigan's fishing streams?

1966. King, or chinook, salmon were planted in 1967. To plant fish means to put thousands of them into the water. This is done by gathering roe, or fish eggs. After the eggs hatch and the fish grow a little, they can be safely moved to a new lake or stream. Large numbers of steelheads and lake and brown trout also swim in the waters.

INDIAN FISHERMEN

In 1836 Indian leaders signed a treaty with the government. It gave them the right to fish in certain waters as they wished. Fish was a major part of their food.

In the 1970s Indians in northern Michigan felt there were too many rules being made. They didn't want rules about how to fish, when to fish, and how much to catch. They felt that the Treaty of 1836 allowed them to fish without these rules.

The matter was settled in court. The court said that the Treaty of 1836 was still a good law. Those Indians whose tribes signed the treaty would be allowed to fish whenever and however they wanted.

How do you feel about this court case? Do you agree with the judge? Why? Talk it over with classmates.

Native Americans fishing in the Great Lakes. What did the Treaty of 1836 guarantee to the Native American fishermen?

JOHN VOELKER, TROUT FISHERMAN

One of the most enthusiastic trout fishermen in Michigan is John Voelker, or Robert Traver. John Voelker is his real name. Robert Traver is his pen name—the one he uses as a writer.

Voelker is a retired justice of the Michigan Supreme Court. He enjoys fishing very much and has a great sense of humor. He has a broad background in law, fishing, and the land of Michigan. For these reasons, Voelker has written many magazine articles, stories, and books. His tall tales about fishing are fun to read.

"I guess one of the big reasons I so much love to fish for wild brook trout in the Upper Peninsula of Michigan, where I was born, is that the trout are so smart they refuse to live in ugly places. So I guess I can't help myself: when I'm out there where trout prefer to live, I'm simply surrounded by natural beauty, I just couldn't escape it if I tried.

John Voelker prepares to cast into one of Michigan's beautiful fishing streams.

John Voelker
January 19, 1986
P.S. And I'm afraid I must confess I don't try very hard."

What do you think John Voelker means by "they refuse to live in ugly places"? How would you describe the place where you would like to fish?

WORDS TO KNOW

STUDY

commercial	license
diet	plant fish
electric screen	pollution
Fish Commission	refrigeration
hatchery	spawning grounds

WHAT DID YOU LEARN?

1. What are three ways to keep fish from spoiling?

2. What is commercial fishing?

3. What did the Fish Commission do to help the industry?

4. What caused poor fishing in the early 1900s?

5. How are the sea lampreys controlled?

6. How are the alewives controlled?

7. What is one duty of the Department of Natural Resources?

8. What law allows northern Michigan Indians to fish as they wish?

USING WHAT YOU HAVE LEARNED

1. How can we keep our lakes and rivers clean for fish and for people?

2. Why were certain nations of Indians allowed to fish without rules?

3. What do you think is the future of fishing in Michigan?

PROJECTS AND REPORTS

1. Prepare a chart showing at least ten fish often found in Michigan waters. Describe each fish and its habits. Draw pictures of the fish.

2. Bring some fishing gear to class and explain its use.

3. Select a library book by Robert Traver. Read part of one of his stories to the class.

4. Try a new fish recipe at home. Explain to the class how it is prepared. Then describe how it tastes.

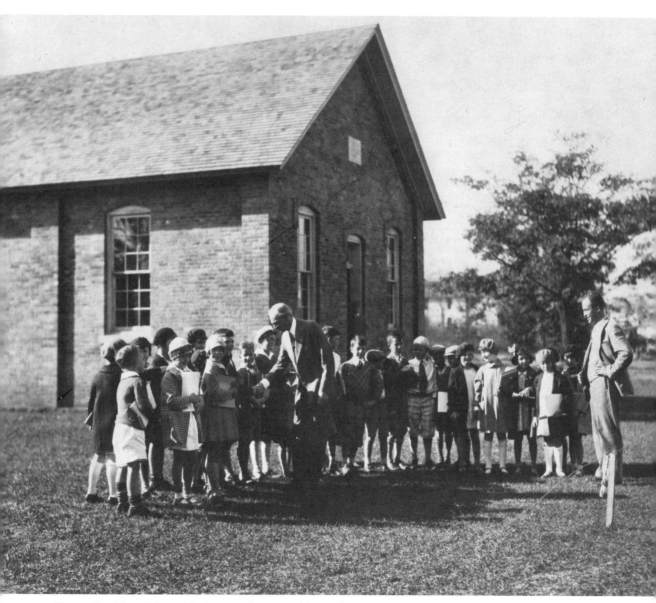

Henry Ford is talking with these students outside the Scotch Settlement School at Greenfield Village in 1929.

Education in Michigan

Education in Early Michigan

Michigan is a leader in public *education*. Even back when the English were in charge, the soldiers' children attended schools. They were taught by traveling ministers and teachers.

In most cases the parents taught their children what they needed to know. They used the Bible to teach children how to read, write, and spell. The children also learned arithmetic.

Mothers taught their daughters how to take care of the home. The girls learned to sew, cook, and clean. Fathers taught their sons how to farm, fish, and make a living for the family.

In the early 1800s many settlers came to Michigan from the New England states. Some of these people had attended schools and colleges. They wanted their children to attend school, too.

Earliest Schools

The early schools were log cabins. Students sat on homemade benches and studied on homemade tables. Later, in *rural* counties, little red schoolhouses were built.

Boys went to school more years than girls did. It was felt

A student's report card from 1881. How does your report card compare with this one?

Entered according to Act of Congress, in the year 1880, by LEVY BROS., Madison, Ind., at the office of the Librarian of Congress at Washington.

RECORD
OF THE STANDING OF
Grade *1*

Ida Hindman *Sept 30* 18*1*.

For the month ending *Sept 30*

	Deportment		95
A	Spelling		102
B	Reading		1
C	Arithmetic		100
D	Penmanship		
E	Geography		93
F	Grammar		
G	Composition		
H	Declamation		100
I	History		100
J	Physiology		78
K	*Algebra*		
L		AVERAGE,	93+

Number Times Tardy

Number Times Absent

D. H. Swann Teacher.

} Parents.

that boys needed *basic skills* such as reading, writing, and arithmetic. Girls didn't need these things to run a home. Students of all ages and grades were taught in one room.

Schools were open only when students were not needed on the farms. Books, pencils, slate boards, chalk, and paper were not easy to get. Many of the lessons were repeated aloud.

Not all children were able to go to school. Many had to stay home and work.

SCHOOL HISTORY

Gather information and pictures about your school. Was your school named after someone? When was it built? What changes have taken place since its beginning? Have any famous people attended your school?

Prepare pictures, reports, and other things that will show the history of your school. Invite other classes to see your display.

ACTIVITY

Arab-American kindergarten students at McDonald Elementary School in Dearborn.

Doherty Elementary fourth grade students in West Bloomfield are studying Michigan history from the same textbook you are using.

Father Gabriel Richard opened a number of schools in and around Detroit during the early 1800s. One school was for *vocational* training of Indian children. The students learned different kinds of work that would help them get jobs. Later Father Richard was one of the *founders* of the University of Michigan.

State School Fund

The Ordinance of 1785 gave money to schools. The money made from the sale of section sixteen of each township was to be spent on education. This money became know as the *state school fund*. The state government gathered the money and then gave it to the townships. It was used to pay teachers, to build schools, and to buy paper and books. City and county taxes also helped pay for Michigan's schools and universities.

Schools in the 1800s

By 1842 over half the schools were open for three months or more during the year. Twenty years later, 75 percent of the children between the ages of four and eighteen attended public schools.

Children were punished for *misbehavior* in school. A good school had order. Everyone did as he or she was supposed to.

Spelling bees, sing-ins, and quilting parties were often held in the schoolhouse during the evenings. The school was a neighborhood center for everyone.

At first, most teachers only had a high school education. The teachers were poorly paid. In 1860 there was one male teacher for every two women teachers. School districts often hired men for the winter term. It was then that the older boys, free from work on the farm, attended school. School terms were short, often lasting only during the winter months.

One school was founded by Laura Haviland, a Quaker. In 1836 she started the Raisin Institute. It was a school to teach hand skills, such as cleaning and sewing, to poor black and white children. The school closed in 1900.

Today little red schoolhouses have been replaced by *consolidated* schools. These are found in the rural parts of the

This painting shows a one-room school, where all grades met together. Do you think you would like a school like this?

counties. They offer the same subjects as city, or *urban,* schools.

Higher Education

The University of Michigan, established in 1837, opened in Ann Arbor in the fall of 1841. There were just six students. This school is now one of the important state universities in the United States.

Michigan State University at Lansing was the first state *agricultural* college in America. Eastern Michigan University was the first teacher training school west of the Allegheny Mountains. Since it opened in 1852, it has had both men and women students.

Central Michigan University was the first college in Michigan to give a diploma to a woman. That was before the Civil War.

A beautiful part of Michigan State University is the Horticultural Gardens. What can be learned from visiting a horticultural garden?

A design on the building wall marks the Kendall School of Design in Grand Rapids.

Dancers, singers, and musicians from the National Music Camp at Interlochen perform at the close of the camp season. High school and college musicians study there under well-known instructors.

Kalamazoo College was the first *private* college in Michigan to allow women students. Soon other colleges followed its lead.

Things to Read

School districts were given money by the state to buy books for school libraries. Now there are many good libraries in Michigan. Schools and colleges have large collections of books and other materials. The William L. Clements Library of the University of Michigan has hundreds of shelves full of books. The Detroit Public Library has thousands of books, magazines, and records.

Automobile companies and newspaper offices also have libraries.

In 1885, a Ladies' Library was established in Ann Arbor.

Doris Biscoe and Bill Bonds report the news on WXYZ-TV.

Michigan Newspapers

A number of daily newspapers are *published* here. The *Detroit News* and the *Detroit Free Press* have the largest number of readers. Since 1990, these two newspapers have merged together to publish one newspaper for Saturday and Sunday. Many towns and cities publish their own newspapers. Does yours?

There are many TV and radio stations in Michigan. Detroit's WWJ began *broadcasting* in 1920. It is one of the world's oldest radio stations.

Michigan is proud of its schools, libraries, newspapers, and television and radio stations.

WORDS TO KNOW

basic skills	founder	state school fund
community college	misbehavior	tuition
compulsory	publish	urban
consolidated	private	vocation
education	rural	

WHAT DID YOU LEARN?

1. What book was used to teach reading in the early days?

2. If schools and teachers were not available, who taught children what they needed to know?

3. How were schools paid for?

4. When was the University of Michigan founded?

5. When did women first get college diplomas?

6. What kind of schools are in rural parts of Michigan?

7. Name four places where libraries can be found.

USING WHAT YOU HAVE LEARNED

1. Should Michigan have a compulsory school law? Why?

2. Should students attend school the whole year?

3. How have schools changed since the early days in the state?

4. By what means can Michigan people gain education?

PROJECTS AND REPORTS

1. Write a story about a day in the little red schoolhouse. Pretend that you are a student in a one-room schoolhouse. Tell about your school day as a fourth grader. What books did you use? What subjects did you study? Did you have art, music, or gym class?

2. Prepare a report on your town's newspaper, radio station, or TV channel. When did it first begin? What are some interesting stories in the newspaper? Which do you think are the best programs on TV or radio? Share your report with the class.

3. Collect old newspapers and compare them to newspapers which are published today. What kinds of stories are on the front pages? What advertisements do you find in the papers? What were the prices of the newspapers?

4. Interview a friend or a family member who went to school at least 30 years ago. What was school like at that time? What changes have taken place since then? You might wish to tape record the interview and share it with the class.

Holland, Michigan, is famous for its tulips. How did Holland get its name?

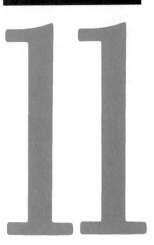

Farming

A Leader in Farming

Michigan is a leader in farming, or agriculture. Michigan grows more red sour cherries and navy beans than any other state. Only three other states grow more fruits and vegetables than we do.

Almost 60 percent of the country's red sour cherries are grown in Michigan. Traverse City is celebrated as the cherry capital of the world. Michigan cherries are even sold in European markets.

The National Cherry Festival is held in Traverse City each July. This is when the cherries are picked. At the festival a cherry queen is crowned and all kinds of cherry treats are sold to visitors.

The soil, amount of rainfall, and temperature chiefly decide what crops will grow in each place. The best farm lands are in the southern part of the Lower Peninsula. About one-third of Michigan's land is good for farming. Some other parts are just right for growing trees.

Indians Were the First Farmers

As early as 500 B.C., the Hopewell Indians farmed in Michigan. They grew corn, squash, and beans.

The National Cherry Festival in Traverse City celebrates cherry-picking time with a parade, games, and other festivities.

Some of the Indians in Michigan during the 1700s grew much of their food. Yet, they still had to hunt, fish, and gather roots, seeds, and berries for their food supply.

Before Michigan became a territory, a few farmers came to Michigan from the East. It was hard for the fur traders and farmers to share the same land. Finally, the fur traders moved west for more furs. Many Indians followed. This left most of the land for the farmers.

After the Erie Canal was built across upper New York State in 1825, a greater number of people came to Michigan to farm. It was easier for them to get here by the canal and Great Lakes water routes.

Early Farming in Michigan

Life was not easy for farmers in the 1800s. They had to find land to settle. Then they had to cut trees and clear the land. Next they built log cabins and made some furniture. They also had to find a way to get food until they could grow their own.

The father, mother, and children had to work together to

stay alive. Neighbors and friends worked together and shared their food in time of need.

Everyone in the family helped with farming. The men and older boys worked in the fields from sunrise to sunset during the growing season. Sometimes children helped with easier tasks.

The women spent much of their day preparing meals. They also knitted, wove, or sewed clothing and took care of children and home. They helped in the fields whenever they were needed.

The work was very difficult. There was no electricity and so, no *appliances*. The mother baked bread. She washed clothes by hand, using a washboard. Water for the wash had to be heated over the wood stove. Buckets of water were brought into the house from a well in the yard. The toilet was outdoors and was called an *outhouse*.

The women usually worked in their vegetable gardens and gathered wild berries in season. They stored food for later use by canning and drying fruits and vegetables. They also made butter and cheese. The farm family was almost *self-sufficient*.

Hay gathering time on the farm.

KEEPING A DIARY

ACTIVITY

Many people kept diaries as a record of their lives. Pretend you are a member of a pioneer family who has just arrived in Michigan from Massachusetts. Write a diary page telling about your trip to Michigan. What belongings did you bring with you? How did you help to get the first crops planted? What kind of work was done by your father, mother, brothers, and sisters? Would you rather be in Massachusetts than in Michigan? Why?

By 1850 Michigan was growing many crops. The farmers were using oxen and horses to help plow the fields and haul the harvest. Large amounts of wheat, corn, and oats were raised. So were rye, barley, buckwheat, and other crops in smaller amounts. Farmers produced wool, butter, and cheese. Sap was gathered from maple trees and made into maple sugar.

Extra crops which the farmer's family did not use were sold for money. The food was sent by train, wagon, and ship to places such as Chicago, Milwaukee, and Detroit. Crops were sent to the East through the Erie Canal.

Farmers Begin to Specialize

In the 1860s the Civil War caused a shortage of workers on farms. Farmers wanted better machinery to make up for the loss of workers. They began to use new machines such as the reaper, mower, cultivator, and thresher. These machines made farming easier but more costly.

Over the next few years, farmers began to grow only one or two crops. A machine that was just right for one kind of crop would not be helpful in harvesting another kind. To get their money's worth out of the machinery, farmers began to *specialize*. They might grow a hundred or more acres of navy beans, sugar beets, sweet cherries, or another crop. Less machinery but more land was needed.

Changes in Farming During the late 1800s

The Union army during the Civil War needed food for the soldiers. To fill this need, great amounts of wheat, corn, oats, and rye were sold to the government. Sorghum was another big crop. Molasses made from sorghum was used to make foods sweet. Food sales to the army became a good business for Michigan farmers.

Thousands of *immigrants* and people from other states came to Michigan for farm work. Others got jobs in lumbering, railroads, building, and mining. There were many jobs in Michigan.

Dexter M. Ferry built a big business. He sold seeds through the mail. By the 1800s Ferry had several hundred workers in his warehouse and on seed farms. Farmers from all states ordered seeds from the Ferry Seed *Catalogs*.

A seed display from the Ferry-Morse Seed Company.

Food Processing in Michigan

Food processing became important in Michigan during the last part of the 1800s. This means changing foods from their raw state to a form that can be stored. (Canning, freezing, salting, smoking, and drying are some ways to process foods.) More sugar beets were grown during the 1890s than ever before. Many sugar beet factories were opened in the Saginaw-Bay City and Thumb areas. Today Michigan is in fifth place in making sugar from sugar beets.

Migrant workers play a big part in harvesting sugar beets and other crops. Migrants are people who go from place to place to help farmers weed and harvest their crops. These people work long hours for low pay. They go back and forth among several states, moving where they are needed as the crops change. Families travel together and work together. Concerned people are trying to improve housing, working conditions, and schools for the migrant families.

Cheese-making factories were built after the Civil War. Fred M. Warner owned a number of cheese factories in and around Detroit. He later became a governor of our state.

All the members of this family are working to pick sugar beets.

With the help of migrant laborers, Michigan's commercial growers harvest thousands of pounds of peppers each year.

ACTIVITY

MAKING CHEESE

Find a recipe for making cheese or cottage cheese. You could get one from the Michigan Dairy Association or from a cookbook.

You might invite someone from a dairy or cheese plant to help you.

Preserving Food

The food *preserving* industry began by drying apples and other fruits. Canning of fruits, corn, tomatoes, and other crops became a huge business. There were almost 100 food preserving plants in Michigan around 1900.

Today freezing is another way to preserve food. Many Michigan foods are quick frozen. What kinds of frozen foods do you eat?

Breakfast Foods

The city of Battle Creek is famous worldwide for its breakfast cereals. Cereals came about because of the Seventh-Day Adventists. People in this church were *vegetarians*. They did not eat meat. Dr. John Harvey Kellogg directed a *sanitarium* (san-uh-TAIR-ee-um) for Seventh-Day Adventists. There he developed cereals for the patients. Many people liked the taste of the cereals and wanted them even after they returned home.

One of Dr. Kellogg's patients was Charles W. Post. After going home, Post was the first to make cold cereals (grape nuts).

In 1906 W. K. Kellogg, brother of John Harvey Kellogg, formed a company to make the dry cereals. Kellogg's corn flakes became the best-selling product of its kind on the market. Today Kellogg and Post are still major food processing companies.

Many kinds of cereals from Michigan are sold worldwide. How many kinds can you name?

An early advertisement for Post Toasties.

LIFE ON A MICHIGAN FARM

What was life like for a dirt farmer's daughter from 1910 to 1930? For me . . . it was walking in my father's footsteps, riding the planker that leveled the plowed ground or on a blanket seat on the tongue of the corn cultivator. . . . On a Sunday my parents and I might go by horse and buggy to visit a relative (no Model T until 1925).

As I grew older, I performed chores indoors and out, feeding the chickens and gathering the eggs, carrying in wood for the kitchen range and in winter for the heating stove in the living room, where we took our weekly baths; pumping water for the cows and horses; raising an orphaned lamb . . . ; doing the dishes and dusting and helping clean, trim, and fill the kerosene lamps, our only source of light till the mid 1920s when we added a gasoline lamp. Some of my girl friends milked cows, but I took piano lessons instead. . . .

The drinking water came from a 20-foot well by the barn. The toilet facilities were the two-holer (which was on occasion tipped over at

Muriel Hunt and her family's farm. How would her life on the farm from 1910 to 1930 be different from your life today?

Halloween time) and a Sears & Roebuck catalog. . . . Later, the family [had] a chemical toilet upstairs.

The basic diet was salt pork and potatoes for breakfast, pancakes or oatmeal, with garden stuff and fruits in season. Chicken and eggs were more for income than Sunday specials.

Though electricity did not reach our area till the mid 1930s, we had had a phone as long as I can recall. We were on a party line with several others, some of whom were very inquisitive.

My pony . . . brought great pleasure, companionship, and cheap transportation for four years of high school and two years of teaching in a one-room country school. . . .

By the way, those two years of teaching [ended] my years on the farm, where, according to today's standards, we lived well below the poverty line. Mother knew it at the time as she had trouble making ends meet. Dad, on the other hand, was repaid watching the seeds sprout and listening to the corn grow on a warm summer's night.

Muriel Wolkins Hunt
Buchanan, Michigan

1. Why do you think people took only weekly baths?

2. What were some jobs for young Muriel on the Hunt farm?

This farmer is plowing in 1920. How has the life of a farmer changed?

Farming in the Twentieth Century

Many people lived on farms at the beginning of this century. They lived in *rural* areas out in the country. The richest farm lands were found in Chippewa, Delta, and Menominee counties. Hay and potatoes were the best crops. Some farmers raised cattle and sheep. Michigan was once an important producer of wool. Today the farmers sell sheep and lambs only for food.

Hard wheat used mostly for bread was one of the chief crops in Michigan. Then other states began to grow more wheat, so Michigan grew other crops, such as corn and vegetables. Today, however, Michigan leads in growing soft white winter wheat used for making cake flour.

Many people also lived in cities. These are called *urban* areas. People began moving from the farms to the cities. Michigan was changing from a rural state to an urban state. Fewer people were making a living by farming.

By 1920 cities were becoming *industrialized*. More people were needed to work in the factories. More homes were needed for the workers, and the cities began to spill over into the farm country. Land for new houses was bought from the farmers.

POTATO DIGGIN' TIME

Potato picking time lasted about two weeks. Schools were closed in the farm counties. Work began at seven in the morning and lasted until sunset. Farmers and their families dug and picked up the potatoes.

In the 1940s, a potato picker might earn 25 cents a bushel. A hard worker could pick about 40 bushels a day. With the money earned, a picker might order clothing and other things from a catalog.

Today machines are used to harvest potatoes.

CASH FROM MICHIGAN FARM PRODUCTS

ACTIVITY

Study the chart of money earned from sales of farm products and answer these questions:

1. What is the most recent year on the chart? What is the oldest year?

2. The chart shows totals for two general categories of farm products. What are they?

3. What single product earned the most money for our state in 1980? in 1990?

4. Which product brought in the second highest amount of money in 1990?

5. Figure the amount of dollars received from fruit in 1990.

6. Did the total amount of money earned from farm products in 1990 rise or fall from 1980? Do you think the trend will continue?

7. What different things help decide how much money Michigan farmers will earn from the sale of their products each year?

MONEY FROM FARM PRODUCTS (in thousands of dollars)

PRODUCT	1980	1990
LIVESTOCK AND PRODUCTS		
Dairy	647,491	640,686
Cattle and Calves	257,567	258,869
Hogs	135,678	193,744
Eggs	57,760	47,237
Sheep and Lambs	5,439	4,565
All Chickens	3,640	2,958
Turkeys	—	31,920
Honey	—	3,151
Other Livestock	29,207	22,518
TOTAL LIVESTOCK & PRODUCTS	**1,137,485**	**1,205,649**
CROPS		
Field Crops and Vegetables:		
Corn	511,355	266,559
Dry Edible Beans	149,250	58,055
Soybeans	227,372	248,899
Sugarbeets	77,004	50,253
Wheat	121,899	85,551
Potatoes	52,606	50,335
Hay	20,210	80,719
Oats	22.011	12,318
Mushrooms	13,049	20,793
Mint	1,498	598
Rye	866	975
Barley	1,332	1,998
Vegetables	123,228	160,251
Other Crops	10,494	14,115
Fruit:		
Apples	48,174	75,818
Cherries	40,593	60,635
Grapes	11,825	13,548
Peaches	7,584	8,028
Strawberries	7,001	6,081
Pears	2,141	2,055
Plums and Prunes	2,550	2,173
Other Fruit	1,030	32,555
Other Products:		
Greenhouse, Nursery	109,767	211,728
TOTAL CROPS	**1,611,153**	**1,464,040**
TOTAL LIVESTOCK & CROPS	**2,748,638**	**2,669,689**

Source: Michigan Agricultural Reporting Service.

Farming in Michigan Today

Life today on the farm is much different than it was at the beginning of the 1900s. There are telephones, TVs, cars, electric stoves, and refrigerators, just as in the city. The farmers, though, still worry about weather, rainfall, and plant and animal *diseases*. The price crops sell for can also be a worry. Prices can change from week to week and from year to year.

Farmers today are better educated in farming. Many have studied in college about soil, animals, and improved kinds of feed. The State Farm Bureau helps to inform farmers about new ways to improve crops.

COMPARING FARM LIFE

ACTIVITY

Prepare a chart showing how farm life has changed because of TV, radio, cars, telephones, and other such things.

Tomatoes must be picked by hand.

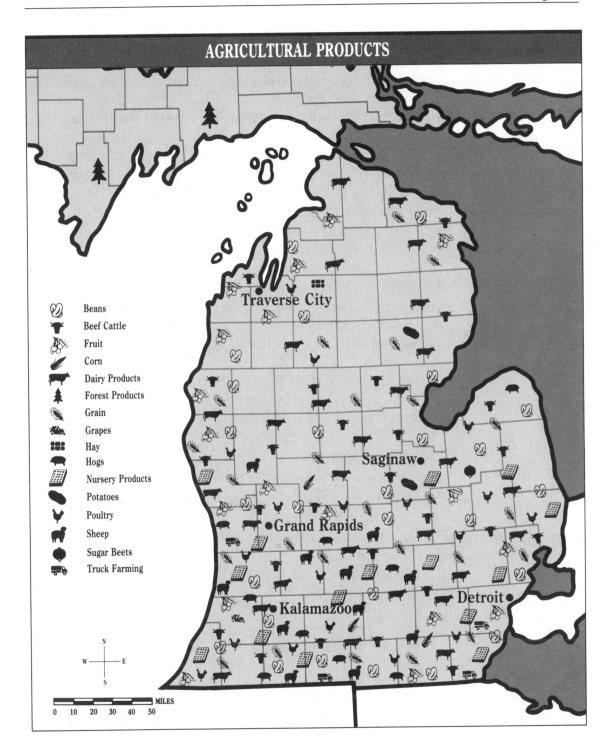

AGRICULTURAL PRODUCTS

Traverse City

Saginaw

Grand Rapids

Kalamazoo

Detroit

Beans
Beef Cattle
Fruit
Corn
Dairy Products
Forest Products
Grain
Grapes
Hay
Hogs
Nursery Products
Potatoes
Poultry
Sheep
Sugar Beets
Truck Farming

N
W E
S

MILES
0 10 20 30 40 50

Michigan's Nursery Industry

Michigan's *nursery* industry is becoming very important. A nursery is a place where plants and trees are raised and sold. Thousands of people order tulip bulbs, flowers, trees, and bushes from Michigan nurseries. Each spring Holland, Michigan, attracts visitors who come to see the hundreds of acres of tulips in bloom. Can you guess how Holland got its name?

Great amounts of spearmint and peppermint were grown in Michigan near Kalamazoo. The mint oil was used in medicines and chewing gum. It was also used in toothpaste flavoring. Today Michigan does not grow as much mint as in the past. But it is still one of the leading states in selling mint oil.

Vineyards

Michigan has many *vineyards*. These are fields where grapes are grown. Paw Paw is the center of a vineyard area. Many kinds of grapes are grown there. A Grape Festival is held each year.

Wines from our state are becoming more and more popular. Now we are the fourth largest wine making state in the country. But most of our grapes are turned into grape juice.

Problems in Farming

Michigan farmers share the same kind of problems as farmers in other states. Some who borrowed money for new machinery or seeds are finding it difficult to pay back their loans. The *interest* rates are high. But farmers have not been getting high prices for their crops.

As farm *profits* fall, some farmers have to sell their land to repay their loans.

The *Detroit News* ran a story about a farmer from Ingham County. Like many other farmers, he borrowed money for his farm in the late 1970s, and now he doesn't have enough money to pay it back. He is a hard worker and has done everything he could to keep his farm.

"I love farming. I feel in a few years down the road this land is going to be worth some money. I might be wrong. It's

Grapes are a major agricultural product grown in Michigan.

just a thought. I'm 51 and almost starting over again, is it worth it?

"I don't want to be like I think a lot of other farmers are, just hang in there and struggle and hope that things are going to get better. But what am I going to do?"

Most Michigan farmers like to farm. They enjoy working the soil and seeing the crops grow. It would be difficult for them to give up their farms. Some farms have been in their families for many years.

Changes in Farms and Farming

Many changes have taken place in agriculture since 1950. There are fewer farms, but the size of the farms is larger. The Michigan farmer grows, on the average, enough food to feed himself and 78 other people. Farming is Michigan's fastest growing industry.

ACTIVITY

URBAN AND RURAL POPULATION IN MICHIGAN

	URBAN	RURAL
1920	61%	39%
1930	68%	32%
1940	66%	34%
1950	71%	29%
1960	73%	27%
1970	74%	26%
1980	71%	29%
1990	70%	30%

Which year had the highest percent of people living in the urban areas? In which year was the highest percent living in the rural areas? Do the figures show a trend? What do you think will happen to the population by the year 1995? by 2000?

STUDY

WORDS TO KNOW

agriculture	migrant
appliance	nursery
catalog	preserve
disease	profit
dirt farmer	rural
food processing	sanitarium
immigrant	self-sufficient
industrialize	specialize
inquisitive	substitute
interest	urban

WHAT DID YOU LEARN?

1. How much of Michigan's land is good for farming?

2. Who were Michigan's first farmers?

3. Who did the work on pioneer farms?

4. What tasks did the women do? the children?

5. What machines made farming easier after the 1860s?

6. How do migrant workers help farmers?

7. What are three ways of preserving foods?

8. How did breakfast cereals get their start?

9. Name ten leading Michigan farm products.

USING WHAT YOU HAVE LEARNED

1. Why are there fewer but larger farms in Michigan today?

2. Do you think Michigan will be an agricultural state in the next century? Why?

3. What problems face today's farmers?

PROJECTS AND REPORTS

1. On a map of the state, show the farming and forest areas.

2. Prepare a report on migrant workers and their families. Where do they come from? How long do they stay in one place? Where do the children go to school?

3. Prepare a report to present to the class on one of the food products in Michigan. Where is it grown? To whom is it sold? How is it processed?

*Before the automobile, people traveled by horse and wagon or buggy. This is
a street in Chelsea around 1900.*

Henry Ford and the Automobile

Michigan on Wheels

A ny customer can have a car painted any color that he wants so long as it is black."
Henry Ford, 1909

Automobile Centers

Before Detroit was known as the "Motor City," the city of Flint was called the "Vehicle City." By the 1880s Flint was one of the biggest makers of wagons and *carriages*. Later, in Flint, Detroit, Lansing, and Pontiac, horseless carriages were made. These cities became famous automobile centers.

Horses had long been important. Farmers needed horses to get most of their tasks done. On the farms and in the cities, horses pulled the wagons and carriages from one place to another. People either went by horse or walked. Then the automobile was invented.

Internal Combustion Engine

Many people think that the automobile was first made in America. But it had its beginnings in Europe. Gottlieb Daimler, a German, invented the *internal combustion engine*. The engine used coal for fuel. An electric spark made the fuel

Flint has continued to be a "Vehicle City."

explode inside a *cylinder*. This made the automobile move. Other Europeans also began making automobiles.

The first automobile in America with such an engine was built in Massachusetts by Charles E. Duryea and J. Frank Duryea.

Autos Come to Michigan

In 1896 the first automobile was seen on Detroit streets. It was driven by Charles Brady King, a *mechanic* who made railroad cars.

Ransom E. Olds, of Lansing, built a gasoline-driven automobile. In 1895 he began to make automobiles to sell. Olds was the first maker of automobiles in Michigan. By 1900 he had sold 500 cars. The Oldsmobile was named after him. A song, too, was written about the "Olds" automobile.

Henry Ford and the Model T

Another young man, Henry Ford, had become interested in automobiles. He was born on a farm in Dearborn. One day, at about age 13, he and his father went to Detroit on business.

On that trip, Henry Ford saw a steam engine running a threshing machine. He wanted to know more about it. This wonderful thing started him on the way to making automobiles.

At age sixteen, Henry Ford left the farm for Detroit. There he worked in a number of jobs. One of the jobs was in a machine shop where he could use his interest in mechanics. His father gave him some farm land near Dearborn. So young Ford became a part-time farmer. The rest of the time he repaired machinery.

A few years later, the family moved to Detroit. Henry Ford then worked as a mechanic. He experimented with engines and auto designs in his spare time.

Henry Ford with the first Ford car and the ten millionth Ford car, a 1924 Model T.

After King's first drive in Detroit, Henry Ford's *quadricycle* was tested on the streets. It worked!

The Ford Motor Company was formed in 1903. In a small factory in Detroit, the first Model A automobiles were *manufactured*. Many Model A's were sold. Later Ford built factories in Highland Park and, finally, on the River Rouge in Dearborn. Today the Rouge plant covers more than a thousand acres.

The successful Model T Ford was introduced in 1908. This automobile "put America on wheels." It changed the way of life for people everywhere. The Model T was made for 19 years. People fondly called it the "Tin Lizzie" because it rattled over the bumpy roads.

FIRST WOMAN DRIVER

One of the first women drivers was Olive LaVigne. She began driving at the age of seven in 1904. There were no rules, yet, about the age of a driver.

Joseph P. LaVigne drove a powerful steam car which took a long time to get up steam. When he came home for lunch, he would leave his car running in the front of his house. Then he could jump into the car right after lunch and not be late for work.

Olive had watched her father drive. One day, when her father began eating his lunch, she got into the car and drove around the neighborhood. She did this often. Finally, her father built her a car in his workshop. (He was an inventor who built hundreds of new things.) The car was called "La Petite," (meaning little). Olive LaVigne drove all kinds of automobiles during her lifetime, even a ten-ton truck her father had built.

Laws on the Use of Automobiles

At first small, round metal tags were used for *registering* cars. This was attached to the dashboard. Besides that, the owner had to have that number painted on the back of his car in figures three inches high.

The year 1920 was the first time license plates with

ROBERT THOM

City streets built for wagons and buggies were soon filled with automobiles. Try to find out which of your ancestors bought the first automobile in your family.

numbers on them were used. Today "Water Wonderland" is also printed on the plate. A person must get a license from the state to drive an automobile.

A law passed in 1905 allowed automobiles to go up to 25 miles an hour on the highway! Eight miles an hour was the top speed in business districts of the cities.

LIST DRIVING RULES

Prepare a list of the rules one should obey when driving a car today. Check with the police department of your city or town. Or get a book of rules from your county offices.

ACTIVITY

Assembly Lines

Henry Ford is known worldwide for building cars on the *assembly line*. On the line, workers did one or two tasks of putting together the automobile. The auto passed in front of them on a *conveyor belt*.

Ford announced, in 1914, that five dollars would be the *minimum* pay for eight hours on the job at the factory. People thought they might be able to buy an automobile if they had such good pay. People from all over the world came to work in the Ford factory.

Other Automobile Leaders

Another leader in the automobile industry was the Buick Motor Car Company. It was started by David D. Buick, a Scottish immigrant. He came to the United States when he was two years old. He lost both of his parents at age five. He worked for a Detroit plumbing supply business. He invented a number of things to improve plumbing until he became interested in automobiles.

By 1931, cars were being built on assembly lines like this one at the Ford Rouge Plant in Dearborn.

In Flint, you can tour a modern automobile plant. Look again at the picture of the 1931 assembly line. What are some changes you can see in the way cars are put together?

William C. "Billy" Durant built the General Motors Company in 1908. Durant was a good businessman. First he made carriages in Flint. Then he began making automobiles in the early 1900s.

There were many other leaders who built automobile companies. The Dodge plant, the Packard plant, and the Jackson plant were some of them. Many of the early companies are not around today.

Busses and Trucks are Made

When the auto plants began building trucks and busses, even more changes took place. Farmers used the trucks to carry their goods to market. People who could not afford their own car could go almost anywhere by bus. At last, a ride in a horseless carriage could be enjoyed by everyone.

Changes in American Life

By 1914 Americans were enjoying the automobile. Everyone wanted one. People in the automobile industry were getting rich. Automobiles helped other businesses to grow. Steel, rubber, gasoline, plate glass, and many other things were needed to make cars.

The automobile changed everyone's life in some way. People traveled from the farm to the city and from state to state. Hotels were needed for overnight trips. Garages and gasoline service stations sprang up in most towns and cities.

Roads were improved and more roads were built. With more cars on the roads, there were often traffic jams. The traffic light was invented to keep order on the streets.

More police officers were needed. They helped keep safety on the roads for both *pedestrians* and drivers.

Auto makers build research cars like this one to learn things about car design and performance. This Probe IV, developed by Ford, is designed to slide through the air with very little resistance.

CHANGES CAME WITH THE AUTOMOBILE

1. **Prepare a list of all the kinds of businesses that have started since the automobile came about. These may be drive-ins, parking lots, gas stations, and many others. Think of companies that depend on carloads and busloads of people to stay in business.**

2. **Make another list of some of the problems which came along with the automobile. Drunk driving, stealing, and reckless driving are a few.**

3. **Prepare a list of all the *advantages* of automobiles. Being able to get someone to the hospital quickly is one good point. Being able to work several miles away from one's home is another. Think of more.**

ACTIVITY

The automobile helped people living in the country feel they were closer to the city. Since people could now drive to work, *suburbs* began to spread. People also began using the automobile for weekend picnics and taking pleasure rides.

World War I

World War I began in Europe in 1914 between Great Britain and Germany. The United States, at first, did not take sides. The automobile factories built the Liberty airplane engine. Our country sold these planes, food, and weapons to several European countries. As time went on, we traded more and more with Great Britain and the countries friendly to her. We traded less with Germany and her friends. Then finally the United States did join the war on the side of Great Britain.

Airways Were Developed in Michigan

Along with ground transportation, air travel also improved. Charles Lindbergh made the first non-stop *trans*atlantic flight from New York to Paris in 1927. He was born in Detroit. He

Charles Lindbergh, from Michigan, was the first person to fly non-stop across the Atlantic Ocean. He flew from New York to Paris, France, in 1927.

flew his plane, the *Spirit of St. Louis*, alone across the ocean.

Today there are a number of airlines within Michigan. Others connect our state with the major airports everywhere in the world.

Gasoline Engines Used on Farms

The automobile soon led to gasoline powered farm machinery. The life of the farmer was changed. Before the 1920s, a large number of farm acres went into food for the work horses. Now, that was no longer necessary.

Look at the chart on the next page. What happened to horses and mules as more machines were used on the farm?

TRACTORS AND ANIMALS FOR FARM WORK

YEAR	NUMBER OF TRACTORS
1930	34,600
1940	66,500
1949	149,372
1959	194,205

YEAR	NUMBER OF HORSES AND MULES
1920	396,000
1959	37,000

What conclusion can you draw from these two sets of figures?

Stock Market Crash of 1929

In the 1920s people had plenty of money. Many *invested* their extra money in businesses and factories by buying *stock*. A stock is a piece of paper showing that a person owns part of a company.

With this added income, business owners were able to improve their buildings and increase production. Within a few years, there were more goods on the market than people needed or wanted. When businesses *overproduced,* they had to cut prices, lower production, and lay off some workers. As more and more people were laid off, they did not have pay checks to spend on buying goods. This made matters worse.

Pretty soon businesses were losing money and some went bankrupt.

What happened to a company's stocks when it went out of business? The stocks became worthless. The investors lost their money. Banks lost customers.

This problem of overproduction had begun shortly after the end of World War I. Farmers had been growing huge crops to help feed the soldiers from our country and others. But when the war ended, farmers did not cut back on their crops. Prices dropped, and they were the first people to lose money.

The stock market was centered in New York City. In 1929 the stock market crashed. This means that the price of stocks went way down. Within a matter of hours and days, people who had put their money into stocks lost all they had. As the news quickly spread, people hurried to the banks. They wanted to get their money out of savings. Many banks did not have enough money to return to their customers. They locked their doors.

This family from southern Michigan was helped with a loan from the Rehabilitation Administration during the depression years.

The Great Depression in Michigan

In 1930 living conditions went from bad to worse. The next ten years would be a very hard time for millions of people. This time is called The Great Depression. A *depression* is a time of little business activity, when many people are out of work.

In the 1930s and early 1940s, millions of people were without jobs. Thousands lost their homes because they could not pay the rent or *mortgage*. Farmers, too, lost their land because they could not repay their bank loans. Some families did not have enough food, warm clothing, or a good place to stay. They felt that life was hopeless.

One thing people could do without was an automobile. When few cars were sold, the automobile factories had to lower the workers' pay. They also had to let some workers go. This was very bad for Michigan, because our state was a leader in making automobiles.

Unions Formed to Help Workers

Life did not improve for the workers. Finally, the government passed a law which gave workers the right to organize *unions*. A union is a group of workers who have joined together to improve their jobs. Workers now could talk about matters with their employers. *Collective bargaining* became an important way to work out problems. This means each side gives in a little until both sides can agree on the matter.

The workers felt their pay was too low. They also felt that the factories were not safe. They thought the assembly line was moving too fast.

It was hard to get all the workers to join the unions. Many were afraid of losing their jobs if they caused trouble. There were many matters on which employers disagreed with their workers. So there were likely to be some bad feelings between workers and managers.

One way workers tried to make changes in their jobs was to go on *strike*. This meant that they refused to work until an agreement was reached.

*Strikers picketing a
Ford Motor plant.
Do you feel that strikes
are a good way to
solve disagreements
between companies and
workers?*

*Strikers have posted a
sign in an auto plant.*

The United Auto Workers, a union, was begun in 1935 by Walter Reuther. He became a leader for the workers who felt that they were poorly paid and unfairly treated. Reuther had worked in the automobile factories for many years. He was a man of ideas and was a good speaker. He wanted unions to push for better education and good health. He favored care for the senior citizens and anything else that would improve the life of workers. Reuther worked for the union until his death in an airplane crash in 1970.

The New Deal

President Franklin D. Roosevelt began a plan to put people back to work in the 1930s. He called it the New Deal. The United States government hired thousands of workers to build roads, dams, schools, and other public buildings. People now had money to pay for food, clothing, and housing. Living conditions began to improve.

The government provided work for jobless people through the W.P.A. program. These workers are repairing a Detroit street in 1935.

Church groups and other citizen groups also helped by giving food and clothing for the poor. Then in 1939, World War II started. A few years later, the United States joined the war. Soon factories were making war goods again and thousands of people were able to go back to work.

STUDY

WORDS TO KNOW

advantage	mechanic
assembly line	mortgage
carriage	minimum
collective bargaining	overproduce
conveyor belt	pedestrian
cylinder	quadricycle
depression	register
internal combustion engine	stock
invest	strike
manufacture	trans (prefix)
	union

WHAT HAVE YOU LEARNED?

1. What city was known as Vehicle City? Why?

2. How did the internal combustion engine work?

3. Who was the first person to drive an automobile on Detroit's streets?

4. When did Ford build his first automobile?

5. Name two leaders in the automobile industry besides Ford.

6. How does an assembly line work?

7. Why did people want an automobile?

8. Who was the first person to fly across the Atlantic Ocean?

9. What happened in 1929 to start the Great Depression?

10. How did the Great Depression affect people and businesses in our state?

11. Why did workers organize unions?

12. What was Roosevelt's plan to put people back to work called?

USING WHAT YOU HAVE LEARNED

1. How did the automobile change our way of life?

2. Would you go into a store if the employees were on strike? Why?

3. "The world community appears to be getting smaller." How would you explain this sentence after having studied this chapter?

PROJECTS AND REPORTS

1. Make models of the earliest automobiles or airplanes and show them in the classroom.

2. Invite a police officer to speak to the class about seat belt safety. Make a poster to show how the seat belt prevents loss of life.

3. Write a story telling what life would be like if there were no automobiles for people to use.

4. Write a report on any of the early leaders in the automobile industry.

5. Interview someone who lived during the Great Depression of the 1930s. Ask them questions about their work and play. Find out what they and other people did to finally get back to work and a normal life. Share your findings with the class.

6. Learn the song "In My Merry Oldsmobile," and sing it for the class.

Many shipwrecks were caused by the rough waters of Lake Michigan.

Shipping and Ground Transportation

Ghost Ships

H ave you heard about Michigan's ghost ships? Stories have been written about shipwrecks on the Great Lakes. During bad storms and strong winds on the lakes, many ships and their passengers have disappeared. Some tales tell us that these vessels have later been seen on the lakes. The ships were being handled by skilled *crews* and captains when they disappeared.

Lately, teams of scuba divers have tried to find some of these lost ships.

THE *KALIYUGA*

O ne story is about the Kaliyuga, *a wooden* steamer *which was built in 1887 at St. Clair. The ship carried iron ore to the ports on the Great Lakes.*

In the fall of 1905, one crew member who lived in Buffalo, New York, had asked for permission to visit his family. The sailor returned to the Kaliyuga *in plenty of time to board ship. But it had left early without him. The steamer had returned to Marquette for another load of iron ore. It locked through the Soo and steamed south onto Lake Huron.*

The Kaliyuga *disappeared and was never seen again. How, why, and where the ship went down is not* *known. The fall storms of that year had sunk or wrecked 27 ships. The sailor from Buffalo was very lucky to have missed the boat.*

Early Shipping on the Great Lakes

When the French first arrived in the Great Lakes in the late 1600s, they used birch-bark canoes and sailing ships. With the aid of French tools and know-how, the Indian canoe was made even stronger and more dependable in the waters.

The French needed to get their fur skins to Quebec and to Europe. They built larger boats with flat bottoms and pointed ends which they used in the New World. These boats were called *bateaux* (bah-TOH). The fur traders came to depend on these boats.

During the 1670s, Frenchman Robert Cavelier de La Salle explored the Great Lakes. His ship was named the *Griffon*, after an imaginary animal that was half lion and half eagle.

The *Griffon*, in 1679, was loaded with valuable beaver furs. It was supposed to sail to Niagara and then return to the mouth of the St. Joseph River. But it never reached Niagara. No one knows what happened to the ship or its *cargo* of rich furs.

Shipbuilding in Michigan

Michigan's forests made shipbuilding a major industry in the 1880s. There was plenty of oak to build strong ships. Towns like Bay City and Saginaw were shipbuilding centers. Marine City was an important shipyard, as was Detroit. Bay City is still building ships today. Algonac and Holland are also making smaller pleasure boats.

Steamships

Beginning in the 1800s ships were built with steam engines. To attract people to Michigan, the steam-powered *Walk-in-the-Water* was built with side-wheelers. (This meant there was

The U.S.S. Michigan *was built in 1833. At that time it was the largest and finest ship on the Great Lakes.*

a paddle wheel on each side.) It carried people, *freight,* and mail. Many more steamboats were then built.

The *Walk-in-the-Water* was wrecked in 1821. The engine was saved and built into a new boat.

Remember how the canal and two locks at the Sault Ste. Marie helped ships? Because of the locks, more ships were needed to carry lumber and minerals to manufacturing centers. Now, it was cheaper and easier to use ships.

In 1833 the steamer *Michigan* was built in Detroit. It was the largest and finest ship on the lakes.

Alexander McDougall of Duluth designed the *whaleback* for carrying ore. The whaleback looked like a huge, floating cigar. Big waves washed right over the top of it and ran off the back. It could stay afloat even in the worst storms. Ships of this kind were in use on the Great Lakes for many years.

These ships were given up as newer and better ones were built. It was important that the ore be loaded and unloaded as easily and quickly as possible.

In 1860 the first *bulk* freighter, the *R. J. Hackett,* was on Michigan's waters. It was built of wood and could carry 1,200 tons. In 1882 the first iron-hulled steamer was built, and it was called the *Onoko.* In 1886 the first steel ship, the *Spokane,* carried ore on the Great Lakes.

We still see freighters on the Great Lakes today. They are built long to carry big loads. When full, an ore freighter looks almost like two smaller ships moving along together. This is because the part in the middle holds the load. It rides very low in the water. The captain's wheelhouse and quarters for the officers can be seen in the front, or *bow,* of the boat. The machinery, smokestack, and cabins for the crew stand high in the back, or *stern.*

A ferry unloading at the Detroit docks in the 1870s.

Large freighters became common sights on the Great Lakes. This is the freighter Cornell *in 1901.*

DRAWING A FREIGHTER

Can you picture what a fully loaded freighter looks like? Draw it on a sheet of paper. Add all the details you wish. If you live where the freighters can be seen, you might wish to take photographs to show to the class.

ACTIVITY

Railroads and Roads Were Needed

Ground *transportation* was needed to carry goods back and forth between docks and factories. Railroads and roads were the answer. Lumber, copper, or other raw materials were some of these goods that needed to be moved from place to place. This meant that roads had to be improved. Railroads had to be built.

Michigan was the first state west of the Appalachians to develop railroads. By 1900, thousands of miles of railroad had been laid.

After the lumber industry used up most of the trees in the state, these railroads were not used as much. Some of the railroad companies tried to get more people to use trains for sightseeing. Their goal was to bring visitors to northern Michigan and keep the railroads alive.

The Great Lakes connected with rivers on three sides of the Lower Peninsula. This presented a problem for through railroad traffic. It was solved by the use of tunnels and car *ferries*.

Robert Thom's painting shows the arrival of the first railroad train at Adrian.

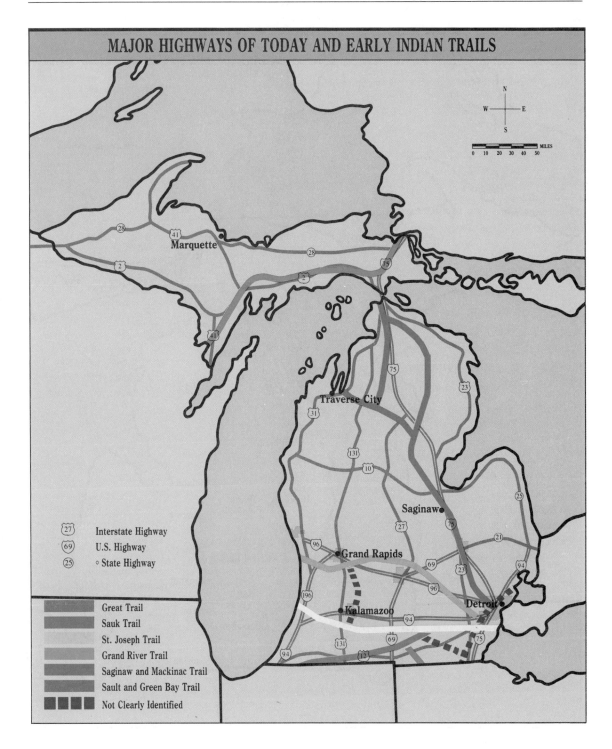

MAJOR HIGHWAYS OF TODAY AND EARLY INDIAN TRAILS

Marquette

Traverse City

Saginaw

Grand Rapids

Detroit

Kalamazoo

MILES
0 10 20 30 40 50

(27) Interstate Highway
(69) U.S. Highway
∘ (25) State Highway

Great Trail
Sauk Trail
St. Joseph Trail
Grand River Trail
Saginaw and Mackinac Trail
Sault and Green Bay Trail
Not Clearly Identified

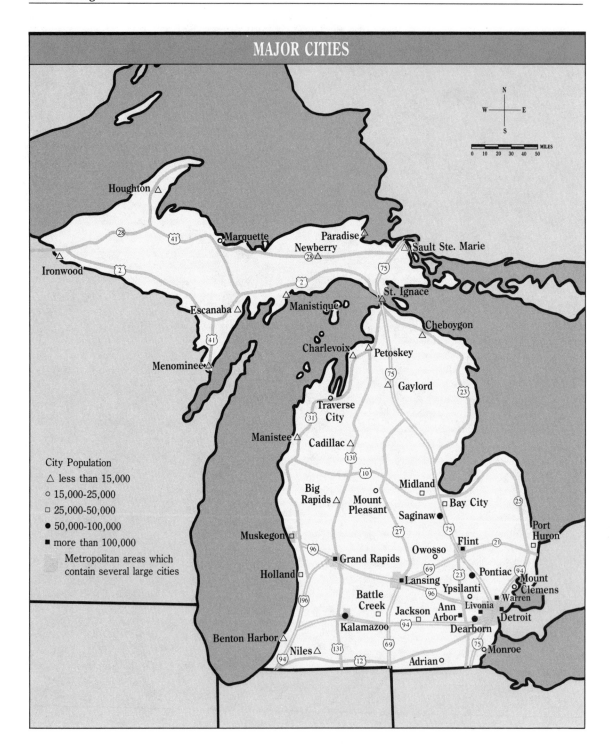

MAJOR CITIES

N
W · E
S

MILES
0 10 20 30 40 50

Houghton △

Marquette ○

Ironwood ○

Paradise △
Newberry △
Sault Ste. Marie △

Escanaba △

Manistique △ ○

Menominee ○△

St. Ignace △

Cheboygon △

Charlevoix ○
Petoskey △

Gaylord △

Traverse City ○

Manistee △
Cadillac △

City Population
△ less than 15,000
○ 15,000-25,000
□ 25,000-50,000
● 50,000-100,000
■ more than 100,000
   Metropolitan areas which
   contain several large cities

Big Rapids △
Mount Pleasant ○
Midland □
Bay City □

Saginaw ●

Muskegon □
Owosso ○
Flint ■
Port Huron □

Grand Rapids ■

Holland □
Pontiac ●
Mount Clemens ○
Warren ■

Lansing ■
Ypsilanti
Livonia ■
Detroit ■

Battle Creek ○
Jackson □
Ann Arbor ■
Dearborn ■

Kalamazoo ●

Benton Harbor △
Niles △
Adrian ○
Monroe ○

Ferries

In 1854 the first railroad line across southern Canada stopped at Windsor. This city was across the Detroit River from Detroit. Ferries then carried passengers and goods across the river.

In 1867 the Great Western ferry was put into service. Passengers could then stay on the railroad cars while crossing the river. Another such service was begun between Port Huron, Michigan, and Sarnia, Canada. Another ferry was open the year round. It ran between Mackinaw City and St. Ignace, across the Straits of Mackinac.

After the Civil War, Michigan's industries grew. The need for shipping and ground transportation became more important to businesses of all kinds.

Ferries have always been an important way to cross water in Michigan. This ferry was operating at Pentwater in 1912.

Soo Canal

In 1942 work was begun on a new and larger lock at the Soo Canal to take the place of the Weitzel Lock. This new lock, named the MacArthur Lock, was finished in 1943. Another one was replaced in 1968. At the present time there are four American locks at the Soo. These are used by ships every day. Thousands of people visit the Soo each year.

Rules for Ships

Today all ships and boats must meet safety rules. All ships and boats must have *life preservers* on board. Each ship must also carry a lifeboat, radio, radio-telephone, and *radar*.

The United States government has done much to improve shipping and recreational boating in the Great Lakes. Each spring the *channels* of the rivers are carefully marked with *bouys*. This tells the boaters where the deepest parts are.

Lighthouses help to protect the ships on the Great Lakes. Lights warn ships that they are getting too close to shore. Lighthouses are built at certain places for the safety of ships. The Au Sable Lighthouse, near Grand Marais, is being *restored* by the National Park Service. The White River Light Station,

This aerial view shows the Soo Locks. You can see how a ship goes from a higher level to a lower level by traveling through the locks. The trapped water between the gates can be raised or lowered to let a ship come in at one level and go out at another.

Sailing is a popular sport in Michigan waters.

Lighthouses like these near Tawas (left) and Sable (right) were helpful aids to navigation on the Great Lakes. Today, most ships rely on radar instruments for safe navigation.

north of Muskegon, has been run for 47 years by William Robinson. The old lighthouse at Presque Isle Harbor, built in 1840, is still standing.

A foghorn also warns ships if they are too close to shore during a fog. The captains of ships today study the weather and storms by using the radio and radar.

St. Lawrence Seaway

In 1954 the United States Congress passed a law that joined the United States and Canada in a waterway project. Together, the countries built a larger and deeper St. Lawrence Waterway. Now larger ships, even from foreign countries, can enter the Great Lakes. The waterway was opened in 1961.

THE WRECK OF THE *EDMUND G. FITZGERALD*

One of these big freighters was the Edmund G. Fitzgerald. *It was the largest ship on the Great Lakes. In 1975 it was caught in* a terrible storm. The ship likely broke in half and sank rapidly. All lives were lost.

The Edmund G. Fitzgerald *did* have a radio, radar, and a lifeboat. Even so, these things did not help to protect the crew from the sudden raging storm.

A song was written telling the story of this ship. It is "The Wreck of the Edmund Fitzgerald" by Gordon Lightfoot.

STUDY

WORDS TO KNOW

bateaux	freight
bulk	life preserver
bouy	radar
bow	restore
cargo	stern
channel	steamer
crew	transportation
ferry	whaleback

WHAT DID YOU LEARN?

1. What are Michigan's ghost ships?

2. Why was the sailor who missed his ship a lucky man?

3. What kind of boat did the French build to carry fur skins to Quebec and Europe?

4. What happened to the *Griffon?*

5. Why was Michigan a good place for shipyards?

6. What kind of ship was built in the 1800s to carry big loads?

7. Why was the whaleback used to carry ore?

8. Why did Michigan develop railroads?

9. Why did Michigan need ferries?

10. Name five safety rules for ships.

11. How does a lighthouse protect ships?

USING WHAT YOU HAVE LEARNED

1. How did shipping help to make Michigan an important industrial state?

2. How can the Great Lakes be made safe for large and small boats?

3. What kind of a state might Michigan have been if we did not have the use of the Great Lakes?

PROJECTS AND REPORTS

1. Read stories about some of the shipwrecks and ghost ships on the Great Lakes. Read or tell one story in class.

2. Make models of canoes and boats used on the Great Lakes. Show them in the classroom.

3. Invite a guest speaker to the class to talk about boating safety. Prepare a list of questions that the class would like to ask.

4. Make a painting or drawing of a ship on the Great Lakes.

5. Find a record or sheet music for "Wreck of the Edmund Fitzgerald" by Gordon Lightfoot. Perform or play the song for the class.

Downtown Detroit ethnic festivals are held every weekend from the first of May to the middle of September. These Ukrainian-Americans are enjoying their festival.

Our Ethnic Heritage

We Have Come From Everywhere

People have come to Michigan from almost every country in the world. We in Michigan are either immigrants or *descendants* of immigrants. The Indians are native Michiganians because they were the first settlers.

This chapter will tell about the background of many groups who live in Michigan. It tells a little of their cultures and *traditions*. All of the ethnic groups have helped make Michigan a better place to live.

Native Americans in Michigan

About 62,000 Native Americans (Indians) live in Michigan. Five thousand or more of them live in Detroit. Some of these people are from other states. They came to Michigan looking for jobs.

Outside of Detroit, some Native Americans could decide to either live on reservations or in small towns and cities.

Native Americans hold many kinds of jobs. A large number of them are *skilled* workers in the *construction* industry.

Native Americans are very good at certain *handicrafts*, which they learn from their nations. Basswood and hickory baskets are some of the things they make. The Native Americans at Mt. Pleasant make snowshoes by hand, as their parents and grandparents did.

Yvonne Walker is an Ottawa-Chippewa artist. She makes beautiful quillwork boxes and other pieces from porcupine quills. She has learned to do this by watching her elders do the same thing.

Harriet Shedawin, a Chippewa, learned to make lovely baskets as a child on Sugar Island. She has been making them ever since. She teaches other Chippewa the art of making baskets so that it will never be forgotten.

EDITH BONDIE, MASTER BASKETMAKER

Edith Bondie, a Chippewa, is Michigan's master black ash basketmaker. One of her baskets is on exhibit at the Smithsonian Museum in Washington, D.C.

The black ash tree grows up to 100 feet tall in Michigan. It is usually found in wet woods and swamps. It is a shade tree and may be seen in different places. The wood is used in cabinet work and in making barrel hoops and baskets.

Edith Bondie does more than weave the traditional basket designs. She also cuts and prepares the black ash splints. First, she soaks the log in water for several weeks. Then she pounds the log with a heavy pole to loosen the strips. The strips are cut and then are ready to be woven into beautiful baskets.

Edith Bondie learned from her grandmother how to make baskets.

Edith Bondie is holding the pieces of wood she will use to start a basket.

French

The first Europeans here were French. After the explorers, fur traders, and missionaries, French families began to come. The city of Monroe, first known as Frenchtown, was settled by many French people. French was the language there for many years. Bay City, Muskegon, and Detroit published newspapers in the French language.

The French were the first to grow orchards in Michigan. It is said that they brought apple trees from France. They also planted pear trees.

Early French enjoyed dancing to the tune of the fiddle. They held a celebration just before the beginning of lent. New Year's Day was another holiday of great joy. A dinner of muskrat meat was often served.

Finnish

Besides working in the mines and lumbering in the Upper Peninsula, some of the Finns wanted to farm. Others opened shops, restaurants, grocery stores, small hotels, newspaper offices, and print shops.

The Finn Fest is held at Suomi College to celebrate the Finnish heritage.

Suomi College in Hancock was founded in 1899 as a cultural center. Here Finns can take part in dances, music, and crafts of their homeland. The Finnish language is also taught at Suomi.

Scottish and Irish

The people from Scotland were scattered throughout the state. Many of them lived in Macomb, St. Clair, Huron, Saginaw, and Alpena counties.

Highland games are still held in Detroit and Alma. During the games the Scots compete against each other in sports, dancing, and bagpiping.

In 1846 the potato crop in Ireland failed. Many Irish came to the United States looking for work and land to farm. A few came to Michigan. If they had stayed in Ireland, they may have starved.

The Irish men worked hard and long hours in building the railroads. Many of the women worked as household servants. The Irish enjoyed music and good friendship.

Immigrants who came to the United States were registered. They had to have someone to sponsor or help them get started in this country.

Germans

Hundreds of Germans made their homes in Washtenaw County. One group of Germans founded the city of Frankenmuth. This city has many shops that sell goods from Europe. Tourists like to go there to buy Christmas decorations and ornaments. While there, people may also enjoy a delicious German chicken dinner and other foods.

Germans came to Michigan because of good farm land and city jobs. They started German bands and singing groups. Germans enjoyed songs and dances of their homeland. They liked to drink bier, eat sauerbraten with pig knuckles, bratwurst (sausages), and dumplings. Germans owned many breweries around Detroit. There were many German clubs and newspapers in Michigan.

Dutch

The Dutch came to Michigan in large numbers. They started the city of Holland and there founded Hope College. Each spring, thousands of people visit that city to see acres and

Wooden shoe dancers during the Tulip Festival, held in Holland each May.

acres of lovely tulips in bloom.

The Dutch were farmers, and they grew celery, which was an important food crop for many years.

Cornish

When copper mines were discovered, Cornish miners came to the Upper Peninsula. They were from Cornwall, England. Because they spoke English, they adjusted easily to their new home in Michigan.

The Cornish were skillful miners. They were nicknamed "Cousin Jacks" and "Cousin Jennies," but no one knows why. They introduced several new foods such as saffron buns, scalded cream, and pasties. Pasties are a mix of beef, potatoes, turnips, and onions inside a crust of pastry. They are still sold in shops in the Upper Peninsula.

Italians

Italians and Slovenes also settled in the copper and iron mining towns of the Upper Peninsula. Some Italians began to grow potatoes and keep dairy herds.

Italians also worked in factories in the Lower Peninsula. Detroit had three macaroni factories. They made macaroni and several varieties of pasta.

Many Italian customs and foods are now part of American culture. Kissing in public between friends was an Italian custom. Can you name other things we got from the Italians?

Italian immigrants later founded two churches in the Upper Peninsula. St. Mary's church was built in Calumet in 1897 and was closed in 1966. The building still stands. Immaculate Conception was founded in 1902 in Iron Mountain.

Italians today have a history of public service in many Michigan cities. There are a number of Italian radio broadcasts out of Detroit.

Growth After the Civil War

After the Civil War, Europeans were encouraged to come by letters sent from relatives in the United States. The letters told about plenty of good jobs and cheap land. The Michigan government also distributed pamphlets to people in New York inviting them to Michigan.

The number of foreign-born people living in Michigan grew every year from 1850 to 1930.

FOREIGN-BORN POPULATION

ACTIVITY

DECADE	NUMBER OF FOREIGN BORN
1940	683,030
1930	849,297
1920	726,635
1910	595,524
1900	541,653
1890	543,880
1880	388,508
1870	268,010
1860	149,093
1850	54,703

- **Which decade showed the greatest amount of increase of foreign-born people in Michigan?**

- **Why do you think so many people came here?**

- **Which decade showed the greatest decrease in foreign-born people? Why?**

After the 1900s, more people came from eastern and southern Europe. Polish, Russian, Italian, Greek, Hungarian, Jewish, Armenian, Syrian, Rumanian, and more people came. They found jobs in many new factories and businesses. They quickly became homeowners.

Greek town in Detroit.

Polish

Americans of Polish descent are Michigan's largest ethnic group. In Poland, many of the people had been farmers. When they came to Detroit, they were able to get factory jobs and do some farming on the side.

The Polish immigrants moved into Hamtramck, near Detroit, between 1900 and 1920. A lot of them worked at the Dodge automobile factory.

A Polish wedding is a joyous time for the bride, groom, and guests. When the bride and groom arrive at the wedding *reception*, they are greeted with bread and salt. This is a wish that there will always be plenty of food in their home. A big meal is served. There is much dancing and singing. The highlight of the wedding party is when the bridesmaids remove the bride's veil.

The Polish have introduced to us *kielbasa,* better known as Polish sausage. Other Polish food favorites are potato doughnuts and duck soup.

In Bronson, Branch County, a Polish Festival is held each August. A polka band and dance contest, Polish costume parade, and dinner of Polish foods are a few of the highlights.

Black Americans

Generally, it is thought that people in Michigan welcomed black Americans. But that wasn't always so.

In the late 1700s Peter Denison, a young black, was given the leadership of a "colored militia." It was feared that Detroit would be attacked by "unfriendly natives." As soon as the Indians were chased into the forest, members of the black militia were again slaves.

Shortly afterwards, Peter Denison escaped. He lived in Canada for several years. Eventually, he returned to Detroit with his family.

Denison's daughter, Elizabeth Denison Forth, later owned her own business. She also held stock in a steamboat company and a bank. She owned her own home. She died one of the richest women in the state.

Black men voted for the first time in 1870. A few years later, John Wilson was elected to the office of *coroner* of Wayne County. He was one of the first black Americans to hold political office. Thomas Crisip became the first black lawyer in a Detroit court of law in the early 1890s.

Elijah McCoy was an important inventor. He received his first patent in 1872. His inventions were used to get oil to moving parts of machines. The McCoy oil cup was in great demand. People asked if a certain oil cup was "the real McCoy." Frederick Jones, another Detroiter, received a patent on the first refrigerator for trucks and railroad cars in 1950.

Blacks have been leaders in public service. For one, Otis M. Smith was chosen to serve on the Michigan Supreme

Court in 1961. In 1976 William Hart was the first black American to become police chief of a large city, Detroit. In 1966 Clara Jones became the first black director of the Detroit Public Library.

There are many black churches in Detroit and throughout Michigan. The churches sponsor concerts, student scholarships, homes for the mentally retarded adults, and many other needed services. A black church is like one big family.

Today there are many black leaders in Michigan. They serve in various public offices. They are poets and artists. They are educators, lawyers, and doctors. Blacks also work in hotels and other service businesses.

Jews

In 1761 the first Jewish settler, Ezekiel Solomon, came to Michigan. Chapman Abraham was Detroit's first known Jewish resident. They were both in Michigan during the Pontiac uprising. Thousands of Jews now live in our state. There are many Jewish *synagogues* in Detroit and other cities.

The Jewish calendar has many religious holidays. Rosh Hashana marks the beginning of the Jewish New Year. This generally comes in September or October. The family gathers for a special meal at home on the eve of Rosh Hashana. The main religious service, though, takes place in the synagogue.

Yom Kippur comes ten days later. It is one of the most important Jewish holidays.

At the beginning of winter, Hanukkah is celebrated for eight days. Candles are burned in a menorah which holds nine candles. Potato pancakes (latkes) are served, and presents are given to the children. This holiday is also known as the Festival of Lights.

Jews have done much for music in our state. When the Detroit Symphony was organized in 1918, Ossip Gabrilowitsch became the conductor. Upon his death in 1935, Victor Kolar took over. At the same time, Mischa Mischakoff was concertmaster. Karl Hass is a well-known radio personality whose broadcasts about music are heard by thousands of people.

The Bavarian Street Band playing at the Bavarian Festival in Frankenmuth.

Jewish leaders are found in education, public service, medicine, and many other fields. For one, Albert Kahn was a world-famous architect. He designed the General Motors Building, Fisher Building, New Center, and others.

Hispanics

Hispanics are people whose native language is Spanish. Most have come from Mexico, Puerto Rico, and Cuba. Hispanics have come to Michigan for the same reasons as other immigrants. As of 1980 there were about 162,000 Hispanics in the state. Most of them live in Detroit, Pontiac, Saginaw, Lansing, and Grand Rapids.

For Mexican children, their birthday is a wonderful day to break the *piñata* (peen-YAH-tuh). It is often a brightly papered

Spanish dancers celebrate the Hispanic heritage.

animal shape filled with candies, fruits, and small gifts. The *piñata* is hung from the ceiling and is moved up by a rope. Blindfolded children try to break it by swinging a stick. After the *piñata* is broken, everyone sings the happy birthday song.

Hispanics from each country have their own music and dances. They celebrate most holidays that all other people do. Can you name some foods that were first eaten in Hispanic countries?

There are many Hispanic leaders in Michigan. A famous artist, Nora Mendoza, was born in Texas of Mexican parents but spent most of her life in Michigan. Nora's mother died when she was four years old.

Nora Mendoza's father was a house painter. While girls of her age played with dolls, she painted with her father's brushes. She knew at the age of eight that she wanted to become an artist.

She works long hours in painting beautiful, colorful pictures. She understands how her people have suffered. She also knows the hopes of the Mexican people because she worked as a migrant farmer. She has drawn pictures for a book on Mexican migrants.

Chinese

The Chinese community in Detroit today is very small. Most of the Chinese families have moved to the suburbs around Detroit.

The first Chinese came to Michigan in 1872. The first woman arrived in 1910. At first the Chinese men went to the Upper Peninsula to work in the mines. They had a very hard time finding jobs.

Many of them took jobs as servants, cooks, and house workers. A few of them were able to open their own businesses. People received good service at Chinese laundries. Many people enjoyed eating in Chinese restaurants.

Chinese dancers perform the ribbon dance at the Far Eastern Festival held in Detroit.

All members of the Chinese family worked to send children to school and college. One Chinese family in Detroit had nine children. Every one of them had a good education. One became a doctor, another a dentist, a third a mechanical engineer. A fourth member of the family became a teacher, another a social worker, and still another a secretary. The remaining members of the family became nurses.

Harry Chung is known as the "mayor" of the Detroit Chinese community. He is a leader who has done much to help other Chinese people when they needed it.

Today some Chinese still own restaurants and other businesses. Many more are studying to become architects, lawyers, teachers, and scientists.

The Chinese hold the Moon Festival and other celebrations in the old Detroit Chinatown. The Moon Festival is held in the summer. Chinese songs and dances are presented. The players in this celebration wear colorful Chinese costumes.

Japanese

The Japanese-American community began near Wayne State University in Detroit after World War II. At first they lived together. As soon as they earned enough money to buy homes, they began to spread out. Most of these people were the second, third, and fourth generations in their families living in America. They knew English. Many did not know how to speak Japanese.

There are over 3,000 Japanese living in Detroit today. Some of these people are permanent residents. Others are living here just for a time. These people are businessmen who have brought their families with them. Japanese companies have sent their managers to United States offices for one to four years. While in this country, the families take part in and learn American customs.

Koreans

The Korean community in the Detroit area is the seventh largest in the United States. Koreans do not tend to live together in neighborhoods. Rather, they are spread throughout the suburbs.

Most Koreans want their children to attend college. Because they enjoy music, the children often play one or two instruments.

Kimchi (KIM-chee) is a favorite dish of the Koreans. It is prepared with cabbage or radishes, preserved in salt. Other seasonings are added, such as sesame seeds, garlic, hot peppers, and green onions. The Koreans also enjoy eating steamed foods. Fish and meat are quite tasty prepared this way. A favorite dessert is fresh fruit. Koreans are known to be gracious hosts.

The Koreans have many holidays, such as the Moon Festival. Then they offer food and wine to their *ancestors* who have passed on. However, most Detroit Koreans only celebrate two holidays. One is their day of independence from Japan, August 15th. The other is Independence Movement on March 1st.

Newest Ethnic Groups

Even today people from other lands move to Michigan. They seek a better life than what they had in their homelands. People from the Philippines, Middle East, Indo-China, and other Asian countries have come since the 1960s.

Filipinos

Filipinos are people from the Philippine Islands. Can you find that place on a world map?

Most of the Filipinos arrived in Michigan after 1965. Many of them were doctors, nurses, pharmacists, teachers, and engineers. However, in order to work at their professions in Michigan, they had to take more college courses and tests. If they didn't have the money to do this, they had to take other kinds of jobs.

When a young Filipino man desired to marry, he paid all the wedding expenses. Since the 1960s the groom and bride share the costs. A church wedding is the choice of most couples. Divorce does not happen often.

Generally, both Filipino parents work. They share the work of caring for the children and the grandparents.

American holiday foods such as turkey, cranberries, and pumpkin pie are added to Filipino holiday foods. Pansit (Oriental noodles) and lechon (roast pig) are eaten on Christmas, New Year's, and Thanksgiving Day. Other important party days are weddings, christenings, and birthdays.

The parties often include native dances, music, and plays. Many Filipinos wear native clothes on Philippine Independence Day, June 12th, and Philippine-American Friendship Day, July 4th.

Arabs

A few Arabs came to work in the automobile factories at the beginning of the 1900s. Many more began to come after World War II and after the Arab-Israeli War in 1967.

The Detroit-Dearborn area has the greatest number of Arabs of any place in the United States.

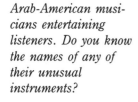

Arab-American musicians entertaining listeners. Do you know the names of any of their unusual instruments?

In Arab neighborhoods, there are coffeehouses and restaurants serving Arabic foods. There are bakeries and stores with groceries and other goods from the Middle East.

There are also several *mosques* (MAHSKS) in and around Detroit. Moslems worship in mosques. Most of the Arabs are Moslems, although some are Christians. Many of the Moslems—southern Lebanese, Palestinians, and Yemenis— have settled in Dearborn.

Indo-Chinese Refugees

About 3,000 Indo-Chinese *refugees* (REF-yew-jeez) settled in Michigan in the 1970s. Refugees are people who leave their countries because of war or political troubles. Nearly all of these people were from Vietnam. A few were from Laos. Sometimes only part of a family came. They hoped relatives could join them later.

Indo-Chinese children learned English quickly. Their parents had more difficulty. Since many of these people had been farmers or fishermen, they had a hard time finding jobs in this state. There were not very many jobs for anyone new in Michigan in the 1970s.

Vietnamese

There are almost 1,000 Vietnamese living in Lansing, Grand Rapids, and Detroit. They had been farmers or fishermen in their homeland. Now they are doing different kinds of work.

The family members are very close. They see value in work. The parents are very hard workers on their jobs. The children put much energy into studies at school.

Hmong

The Hmong farmers lived in the mountains of Laos before they came to Michigan. They speak Hmong. This language was only spoken until the 1950s. Then someone figured out a way to write it. Almost 1,500 Hmong have come to Michigan and are living in Detroit, Lansing, and Grand Rapids.

They have worked hard to learn English so that they could get jobs. Many of the women help their families by sewing and selling pand-dao (PAN-daouw). These are beautifully stitched pieces of *applique* (AP-lih-kay). The women often use bright colors against a black or navy blue background.

Laotians

Laotians settled in the same cities as other Indo-Chinese peoples. They were also farmers who had to learn English to be able to get jobs to support their families.

The Laotian family generally includes the parents, a married daughter and her family, and the other unmarried children. They often live together in one house.

Education is very important to the Laotians. The children are encouraged to do well in school.

Summary

The number of immigrant families in Michigan has been growing. People have come, and are still coming, from all parts of the world. Many schools offer *bilingual* programs. Children who speak another language are given extra help to learn English. Some lessons are taught in their own language. The adults may take evening classes to learn English as a second language.

Immigrants today have to be creative about finding jobs for themselves. Many of them run small stores, restaurants, and gasoline stations. Others find jobs as laborers. The Indo-Chinese and many others have set fine examples of hard work for us to follow.

In this chapter we have talked about people belonging to ethnic groups in Michigan. There are many more groups which have not been mentioned. Besides seeing the importance of the group, we also see the importance of each person. Everyone adds something different and special to our Michigan community. We like people for who they are. It is important for people to be proud of their ethnic groups. It is also important for people to be liked just for being themselves.

What do you think is the best thing about you? How are you different from everyone else? How are you the same as everyone else?

Hart Plaza in Detroit where the festival programs are held.

STUDY

WORDS TO KNOW

ancestor
applique
bilingual
construction
coroner
descendant
ethnic
handicraft

highland games
model
mosque
piñata
reception
refugee
synagogue
tradition

WHAT HAVE YOU LEARNED?

1. Who were the first people living in Michigan?

2. Who grew the first orchards in Michigan?

3. Where is Suomi College? Which ethnic group started it?

4. Why did the Irish come to Michigan?

5. Why do people enjoy visiting Frankenmuth?

6. From where did the Cornish miners come?

7. What are pasties?

8. Why did people want to work in the automobile factories?

9. Why did people from eastern and southeastern Europe have a more difficult time adjusting to life in Michigan?

10. Why did immigrants attend night school?

11. What does the term "the real McCoy" mean?

12. Where do Jews worship?

13. Where do Moslems worship?

14. What do Hmong women make and sell?

USING WHAT YOU HAVE LEARNED

1. How can immigrants be made to feel more welcome in Michigan?

PROJECTS AND REPORTS

1. Interview an immigrant. Where did the person come from? Why? What things does the person like about life in Michigan? How are things different for the person in his or her new home? Share the information with your class in an oral report.

2. On a map of the state, show where groups of immigrants settled in 1850, 1920, 1940 and 1980.

3. Visit different religious centers. Take pictures of the buildings. Learn something about their history. When were they built? Who were the first members? What meetings, or services, are held in the buildings?

4. Prepare a report on ethnic groups in your community which were not covered in this chapter.

5. Prepare a display of any ethnic culture. Show clothing, arts, or foods. Tell the class about the things and how you found out about them.

An aerial view of Detroit, the largest city in Michigan.

Detroit, Michigan's Major City

Detroit, the Motor City

Today most people in Michigan live in the cities. Detroit is the largest city in the state. Over a million people live there. Detroit is in the center of many other cities, or suburbs, of smaller size. Detroit and its suburbs are known as *metropolitan* Detroit.

This area includes Wayne, Oakland, and Macomb counties. People in these counties attend many events in Detroit. The Detroit Institute of Arts, Detroit Symphony, Detroit Tigers, and Detroit Lions are well known. Many conventions are held at the Renaissance Center in Detroit.

Detroit has many offices, factories, stores, schools and universities, hospitals, and research centers that attract people. World headquarters for major automobile companies are located in Detroit. Many skilled and trained people work in Detroit.

Early Detroiters

Detroit's history began in the early 1700s. In 1701, a great many years before the Revolutionary War, Antoine de la Mothe Cadillac built Fort Pontchartrain. He wanted to build a French settlement in Detroit. He wanted French families to make Detroit their home.

That fall, Cadillac's wife and another woman came to Fort Pontchartrain. The people living in the fort were farmers who had been given land to farm. The shape of each farm was long and narrow. Because of this, the farms were called the French ribbon farms.

Cadillac was not able to get many French people to come to Detroit. But he did get about 2,000 Indians to settle around the fort in small villages.

After Cadillac left in 1710, the population of Detroit *decreased*. In 1760 Detroit came under English rule. This continued until 1796 when Americans came to Detroit.

In 1796 about 500 people lived in Detroit. Most of them were French. They spoke the French language and attended the Roman Catholic church. Gratiot, St. Aubin, St. Antoine, Orleans, and Beaubien are a few Detroit street names. These

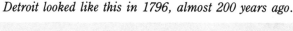

Detroit looked like this in 1796, almost 200 years ago.

and many others are named after early French farmers and settlers.

Detroit Becomes a Town

Michigan was a part of the Northwest Territory until 1880. Then it became part of the Indiana Territory, with Detroit as its capital. Detroit was still a small trading town.

In 1805 a great fire destroyed everything in Detroit. Judge Woodward, an officer in the territory, had ideas for a new Detroit. An architect drew a plan.

When Detroit became a town, the citizens passed some laws. One was that all citizens had to help put out fires. When Michigan became a state in 1837, Detroit had nearly 10,000 people.

By 1880 there were many neighborhoods in Detroit. The Irish lived in a certain place and the Polish in another part of the city. The blacks were in a section known as "Kentucky." The wealthy people lived in an area west of Woodward Avenue and north of Grand River. It was called Piety Hill. Today there are still some *ethnic* neighborhoods in Detroit and other large cities. They aren't as clearly separated as in early years, however. Which ethnic groups live in your community?

Detroit Under Mayor Pingree

Hazen S. Pingree served as mayor of Detroit from 1890 to 1897. He was a very interesting person. He was a native of Maine who was put into prison during the Civil War. While in prison he met some men from Michigan. They couldn't say enough about how wonderful Michigan was. After hearing them, Pingree decided that he would make Detroit his home. When he was released, he went to Detroit and got a job in a shoe factory. Later he founded his own shoe factory.

Ping, as he was fondly called, is known as Detroit's "Reform Mayor." He felt city government was charging the citizens too much for some services. He reduced the gas rates and the fares on the streetcars. Street lighting was made part of the city's responsibility during his term.

"Ask your dealer for them and keep asking him until you get them," says this advertisement for Pingree's shoes.

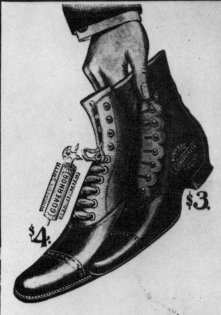

Pingree
Shoe Talk

A metropolitan retailer who has sold large quantities of our shoes (Women's, Men's and Children's) was asked what impressed him most in "Pingree" shoes. He replied: Two things. First, they have a strong individuality — a style peculiar to themselves. Second, they DO wear like iron.

All genuine "Pingree" shoes bear our name; if in addition you see the following trade names stamped on the soles of them, you can positively depend on getting the best shoes ever made for these prices.

"GOVERNOR"   **"COMPOSITE"**
For Men, $4 $3 For Women

These are special examples of "Pingree" shoemaking. At same prices there are no other shoes so good. They come in all reliable leathers, newest shapes and in various weights, adapted for all occasions, from social functions to street wear.

ASK YOUR DEALER for them and keep asking him until you get them | Write us for Catalog and other information

Detroit went through a time of unemployment in the 1890s. Pingree had the front yard of the city hall and other public lands plowed. There, poor people were allowed to grow vegetables. These gardens were known as "Ping's Potato Patches."

Mayor Hazen Pingree in one of "Ping's Potato Patches."

Detroit's Population Increases

During the last part of the 1800s and the early 1900s, Detroit's population grew. Detroit's location in southeastern Michigan was ideal for growth. Can you list some reasons why? Look at a map of Michigan for clues.

Detroit was near the sources of raw materials needed for manufacturing. Lumber, copper, and iron ore were easily brought by rail or water to the many new factories in Detroit. There the factory workers made the raw materials into products that people needed and wanted.

Detroit was also near the major markets where the products were sold. Food and other supplies needed by the workers and their families were also easily brought to Detroit.

DETROIT IN THE EARLY 1900s

There were no paved roads, but there were railway tracks on Woodward, Michigan, and Jefferson avenues. The fares on the Sherman line were three cents from the city hall to the end of the line.

Women were expected to stay home and take care of the house.

They took care of the yards with hand-powered grass cutters and rakes.

When the bicycles came, it was shocking to see any lady trying to ride something made just for the men. Even horseback riding by nice ladies was very bold.

Almeda Raths, 1883-1986

Mrs. Almeda Raths was one of many senior citizens who volunteer to help in the community. Mrs. Raths was giving her time to read stories to school children when she was 103 years old.

Woodward Avenue in Detroit about 1918. What things do you see in this photograph that you would not see in the city today?

Mayors Couzens and Murphy

James Couzens became mayor of Detroit in 1919. He was a close friend and business partner of Henry Ford. Couzens fought against *utility* companies. These were gas, electric, and street-railway services. Their rates were too high. So in 1921 the city of Detroit became the owner of the street-railway company.

Like Pingree, Couzens worried about unemployment. He felt that the city should care for people out of work. He began a plan of public *relief* for the poor.

Frank Murphy served as mayor of Detroit from 1930 to 1933. He, like Pingree and Couzens, wanted to improve life for people. He made up his mind that no one would starve in Detroit. He spent money for food and opened a warehouse where homeless men could sleep. Murphy served during the Great Depression, when thousands of people were out of work.

Murphy allowed citizens to plan outdoor meetings so hundreds of people could meet together. This was because he believed that everyone had a right to speak about their ideas.

Frank Murphy later became governor of Michigan and held several U.S. government posts. One of these was justice of the United States Supreme Court.

During his time as governor, Murphy helped to settle many strikes in the automobile factories. He also helped unions get started.

Blacks in Detroit

Many blacks came to work in Detroit factories. They lived in certain parts of the city where other black families lived. Many blacks worked in the factories.

Black Population in Michigan

YEAR	BLACKS IN MICHIGAN	BLACKS IN DETROIT
1840	707	193
1850	2,583	587
1860	6,799	1,402
1870	11,849	2,235
1880	15,100	2,821
1890	15,223	3,431
1900	15,816	4,111
1910	17,115	5,741
1920	60,082	40,838
1930	169,453	120,066
1940	208,345	149,119
1950	442,296	300,506
1960	717,581	482,229
1970	991,066	660,428
1980	1,198,710	758,939
1990	1,291,706	777,916

What do these numbers tell us about the population of blacks in Michigan and in Detroit?

MAKING A BAR GRAPH

 ACTIVITY

Make a bar graph showing the increase in the number of blacks in Michigan and in Detroit. Record the information in *decades* (ten-year periods) from 1900 to 1990.

The Case of Dr. Sweet

In 1925 Dr. Ossian Sweet, a black *physician,* bought a house for his family in a white neighborhood. After he had moved in, a mob of whites began throwing rocks at his home. Someone inside the house fired into the crowd, killing two people.

Sweet and his family were arrested and charged with first-degree murder. The case was heard before Judge Frank Murphy. The Sweets were found not guilty. The white jury thought that the Sweets had a right to protect their home. Clarence Darrow, a well-known lawyer, defended the Sweet family. Judge Murphy won a *reputation* as being fair in matters of *minority* rights.

Prejudice Leads to Fights in 1943

In the 1940s blacks and whites were competing for the same factory jobs in Detroit. A few people used this to stir up racial prejudice.

When people could not get jobs, they became angry. In early summer 1943, fights broke out between white and black youths on Belle Isle, a city park. The fighting spread to other places until some people were killed or injured.

Many people felt something should be done to end unfairness in hiring and firing workers. R. J. Thomas was then president of the United Automobile Workers. He asked that more housing and parks be available for minorities.

Living Conditions Improve

In 1943 a biracial committee was formed. In 1955 a Fair Employment Practices Act was passed. A government commission was set up to see that people were hired and fired fairly, not because of race.

The number of black people in Michigan grew. Detroit's population was about 30 percent black by 1960. In Detroit and other cities, thousands of blacks were able to get better jobs. Many became teachers, police officers, trained craftsworkers,

A Thanksgiving Day parade is held in Detroit each year.

and professionals. Still, black families could not live where they wanted to.

By the 1960s life was good for many people. But some people in Michigan were still poor.

1967 Riots

Another riot took place in Detroit in 1967. Fighting began and did not stop until the federal troops were sent in to help the Detroit police. There was fighting in other cities in Michigan, too.

A civil rights demonstration in Detroit. Do you recognize anyone in the demonstration?

The New Detroit Committee was formed. J. L. Hudson, Jr., was the chairman. Work was done to get more jobs and better jobs for the poor. By 1968 nineteen cities had passed laws against discrimination in housing.

Detroit Becomes a "Central City"

Today Detroit is sometimes called the "central city." After World War II, Detroit was overcrowded. Because few new houses were built in the city, many people moved to the suburbs. A good number of these were young families. They were also people who could afford to buy new homes.

Many factories, offices and businesses moved to the suburbs where their customers lived. New shopping centers were built which, in turn, drew more people to the suburbs. These same changes happened in other cities in Michigan and the United States.

Detroit has continued as a center for business and culture. It has excellent roads and highways. It still has raw materials for industry and manufacturing. Most important, there are many skilled workers living in Detroit.

Yet, Detroit, like other cities, still has many problems. More poor people and senior citizens live in Detroit who need help. Crime and unemployment are other problems which need attention. The government is trying to improve housing and services to make living and working in the city more desirable.

First Black Mayor

Coleman A. Young, after serving in the state Senate, became the first black mayor of Detroit in 1974. He and his family moved to Detroit from Alabama in 1923. He was just five years old. He attended schools in Michigan and did very well. Yet, he could not get a *scholarship* to go to college.

Young attended trade schools and worked in many jobs. At the automobile factory, he became a union organizer. He spoke out to defend the rights of factory workers and all

Coleman A. Young was elected the first black mayor of Detroit in 1974.

blacks in general.

Mayor Young has said that "the problems of the cities cannot be *isolated* from the survival of the nation." What do you think that statement means?

Other Leaders in Detroit

The first black Superintendent of Schools, Arthur Jefferson, was appointed in 1975. Since 1989 John W. Porter, also black, has been serving as Interim General Superintendent for the Detroit Schools.

Many men and women serve in Detroit and other Michigan cities. Some of them are lawyers, councilpersons, judges, and public officials. John Conyers and George W. Crockett, Jr., serve in the United States Congress from Detroit. Maryann Mahaffey has served on the Detroit Council for many years.

The Detroit Institute of Arts has a collection of paintings, sculpture, and other arts which can be enjoyed by everyone. What can you learn by visiting museums like this one?

DETROIT'S POPULATION

Study the chart which follows. It tells some things about Detroit's population.

EIGHT LARGEST MICHIGAN CITIES

CITY	POPULATION	PERCENT BLACKS	PERCENT HISPANIC	PERCENT UNDER 18	PERCENT OVER 65
Detroit	1,203,000	63%	2%	30%	12%
Grand Rapids	182,000	16%	3%	27%	13%
Warren	161,000	—	1%	28%	8%
Flint	160,000	41%	2%	32%	10%
Lansing	130,000	14%	6%	29%	9%
Sterling Heights	109,000	—	1%	34%	4%
Ann Arbor	108,000	9%	2%	19%	6%
Livonia	105,000	—	1%	28%	8%

1. Which city is the largest?
2. Which city has the greatest percentage of black citizens?
3. Which city has the greatest percentage of Hispanic citizens?
4. Which city has the greatest percentage of people eighteen years and under?
5. Which city has the greatest percentage of people sixty-five years of age and older?

Cities in Michigan, such as Flint, Kalamazoo, Grand Rapids, and Benton Harbor, have important leaders and interested citizens. Each city and town is trying to treat people fairly.

What can you do to help make your community a better place to live?

STUDY

WORDS TO KNOW

biracial
decade
decrease
discrimination
ethnic
isolate
metropolitan
minority

physician
prejudice
professional
relief
reputation
riot
scholarship
state of emergency
utility

WHAT DID YOU LEARN?

1. What is Detroit and its suburbs called?

2. Who founded Detroit?

3. Why did the city of Detroit have fire rules as soon as it became a town?

4. Why were "Ping's Potato Patches" important to Detroiters?

5. According to Mayor Couzens, who should care for the poor?

6. What other government job was held by Mayor Frank Murphy?

7. Why is Detroit's location important?

8. What were some causes of riots in Detroit?

9. What has been done in Detroit to prevent race riots?

10. Name two leaders who worked for better jobs and fair treatment for blacks.

11. Who was elected mayor of Detroit in 1974?

USING WHAT YOU HAVE LEARNED

1. What can citizens do to improve conditions for living and working in Michigan?

2. What are some advantages to living in the city? in the suburbs? What are some disadvantages of each? How can life be improved in both the city and the suburbs?

3. How can we do away with prejudice?

PROJECTS AND REPORTS

1. Make a model of your community as it was 50 or 100 years ago. How is it different today?

2. Prepare a bulletin board about leaders in your community.

3. Make a list of cultural events you might attend in your community.

The mayors of Detroit and Windsor meet at the Freedom Festival, an event celebrated by both cities.

Our Neighbor, Canada

Two Friends

Michigan and Canada are close neighbors. The land and waters of Michigan touch the land and waters of Canada. The boundary between Canada and the United States is the world's longest *unguarded border*.

Every year in early July, people in Michigan and Ontario hold the *International* Freedom Festival. It takes place in Detroit and Windsor. At that time, people promise to carry on their friendship and *cooperation*.

Crossing Over

The study of Michigan is not complete without Canada. People from Michigan do move easily into Canada to visit friends, to shop, work, and enjoy the *scenic* beauty.

In turn, Canadians come to Michigan for the same reasons. In fact, many people in Michigan are former Canadians who left Canada for better jobs. Canadians attend Tigers baseball games, Lions football games, and other sports. They enjoy the musical programs and plays in Michigan.

Students from Michigan sometimes attend college in Canada. And sometimes Canadian students cross the bridge to attend schools in Michigan.

Bridges and tunnels have been built between Canada and the United States. Canals have also been built. These canals connect the St. Lawrence River with the Great Lakes. The canals are part of the St. Lawrence Seaway. A ship can leave Detroit and travel by water routes through Canada to the Atlantic Ocean.

Similarities Between Us

Canada is divided into provinces and territories instead of states. Ontario is the Canadian *province* nearest Michigan.

There are many *similarities* between people in Michigan and in Canada. Most Canadians speak English. But in the Quebec province, French is the language most used. People in Canada have many of the same *customs* and holidays we do. They have a *democratic* form of government. Their standard of living is quite high, compared to other countries of the world.

Canada, too, has Indians. There are also people who were immigrants, or whose grandparents were. Canadians' backgrounds are from Europe, Asia, and many other countries of the world.

Canada is rich in natural resources. Like Michigan, it is one of the world's leaders in industry.

Canada and the United States are each other's best customers. About two-thirds of Canada's trade is with the United States. Canada sells us things such as petroleum, newsprint paper, automobiles, and automobile parts. The United States sells Canada cars, automobile parts, machines, and other goods.

Canada is the largest country in North America. It is the second largest country in the world. Only the soviet Union is larger than Canada. Yet, the population of Canada is not very large. Most of its 26 million people live in southern Canada, near the border of the United States.

Some of the Great Lakes serve as a boundary between Michigan and Canada. The Detroit River, which connects Lake

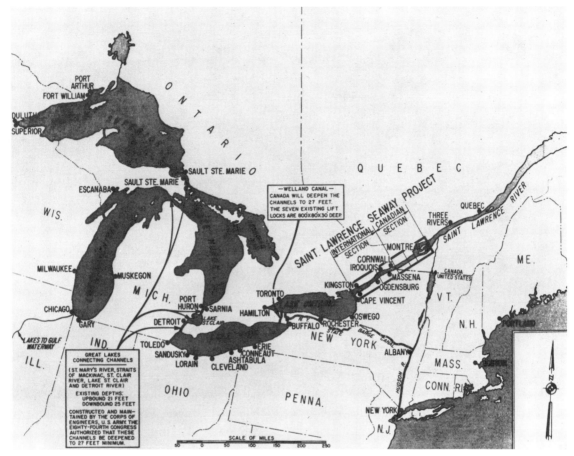

This map shows the St. Lawrence Seaway Project which involved the United States and Canada.

Erie and Lake St. Clair, is also a boundary between Michigan and Canada. This is the only place where a part of Canada is south of United States land.

Across the Ambassador Bridge

From Detroit, one can either take the Ambassador Bridge or the tunnel to Windsor, Canada. It takes but a few minutes to go through *customs*. Customs officers check people who wish to cross the Detroit River. They ask where you were born and if you are a U.S. citizen. This helps them keep track of

You can travel from Detroit to Windsor, Canada, over the Ambassador Bridge.

visitors. (Guns, certain foods, and drugs may not be taken across.)

After passing through customs, cars are allowed to cross the Detroit River. Windsor has many factories. The Windsor Art Gallery shows works by Canadian artists. The Peace Fountain can be seen in a river-front park. This is one of the largest floating fountains in North America.

Not far from Windsor is Amherstburg. In Amherstburg a visit to Fort Malden and the North American Black Historical Museum is an interesting trip. One can discover more about the history of Detroit and Michigan, as well as Canada. One of the battles for Detroit was fought at Fort Malden.

A Windsor street. Canada looks almost the same as the United States. If you have been to Canada, what were some things you saw there that were different than in the United States?

Fort Malden, an interesting place to visit, is located in Amherstburg, Ontario.

The Blue Water Bridge.

Across the Blue Water Bridge

Port Huron, Michigan, is connected to Sarnia, Ontario, by the Blue Water International Bridge. Port Huron is one of the oldest settlements in Michigan. Sarnia is a manufacturing city known as "Chemical Valley." It has oil *refineries* and chemical factories.

Across the International Bridge

The third bridge is between two cities which face each other across the St. Mary's River. Both cities are called Sault Ste. Marie. They are joined by the International Bridge. Sault Ste. Marie is the oldest city in Michigan. It was first visited by Etienne Brulé, who was hoping to reach Lake Superior. Sault Ste. Marie was an important trading post.

The first missionaries arrived in Sault Ste. Marie in 1641. The first mission was begun in 1668 by Father Marquette and

The International Bridge.

Father Dablon. They named the town in honor of the Virgin Mary.

Shared Problems

Sometimes there are disputes between our two countries. One is the worry about what *acid rain* does to the lakes, rivers, and plants. Canada and Michigan both have many factories and industries which burn coal. This is how they make heat or power. It is thought that the chemicals from the burning coals, when joined with rain, make a poisonous acid. This pollutes the waters and the air.

The Peace Fountain in Windsor stands for the peace and friendship which exist between the United States and Canada.

PROBLEM SOLVING

ACTIVITY

- Perhaps acid rain is our major shared problem. Talk about it with a group of classmates. Try to find ways Michigan and Ontario could work together to overcome this problem.

- Do you think a *mass transit* system between Michigan and Canada would be a good idea? (This would be a network of buses or trains.) What are your ideas for the best kind of system?

The people of Michigan have been living with the Canadians in peace for many years. Through cooperation, we can carry on this friendship.

WORDS TO KNOW

STUDY

acid rain

cooperation

customs

democratic

international

mass transit

populate

province

refinery

scenic

similarities

unguarded border

WHAT DID YOU LEARN?

1. Why should we study about Canada?

2. How is Canada similar to Michigan?

3. How is Canada different from Michigan?

4. What are the names of the three bridges between Michigan and Canada?

5. What is the St. Lawrence Seaway?

6. What is acid rain?

USING WHAT YOU HAVE LEARNED

1. How can we better know Canada?

2. How can we solve some of our problems with Canada?

PROJECTS AND REPORTS

1. On a chart, list how people in Canada are the same as people from the United States. List how they are different.

2. Write letters to fourth grade students in Ontario, Canada. Tell them about your school and community. Address the letters to an elementary school in Ontario and to the attention of the fourth grade teacher.

3. On a map of Canada, find the connections between Canada and the United States. Name the bridges and tunnels which can be used to cross over.

4. On a map of Ontario, show the large cities and lakes.

*Ralph Bunche of
Detroit won a Nobel
Peace Prize in 1950.*

Noteworthy Citizens of Michigan

Our People Make Us Proud

I t is hard to list certain persons as being the only leading citizens of Michigan. There are now, and have been in the past, hundreds of such people.

People in Michigan have earned national and worldwide reputations. Some have been in the *arts*. This means writing, music, drama, and painting. Other people have become well known in sports and the business world. Public service, medicine, and education are some of the many other fields with well-known Michiganians.

Outstanding Citizens in Public Service

Ralph Bunche received the Nobel Peace Prize for bringing about a settlement of the Palestinian War. This was a war between Israel and the Arab states. Bunche was one of the leaders who helped set up the United Nations.

Gerald R. Ford was the thirty-eighth president of the United States. Before that, he had been a Michigan congressman for a number of years. He was highly respected by members of both political parties for his fairness and hard work.

The Gerald R. Ford Museum in Grand Rapids. What kinds of information can be found at a presidential museum or library?

The Gerald R. Ford Museum in Grand Rapids houses information about his life. Also, the Gerald R. Ford Library in Ann Arbor has books and journals. These tell about his life in public service.

Martha W. Griffiths wanted to become a *journalist.* Later she decided she was more interested in law. Griffiths was the first woman lieutenant governor in our state. She served under **Governor James J. Blanchard.**

Griffiths felt strongly the need for women to take an active part in government. She served in the Michigan legislature. She was the first woman judge and recorder of Detroit's Recorder Court. In 1955 she was chosen for a seat in the U.S. Congress. She served there for 20 years. While there, she presented the Equal Rights Amendment. This was a bill to give women rights equal to men's.

On November 2, 1982, Martha Griffiths became the first woman to be elected lieutenant governor of Michigan.

William Milliken served as governor of Michigan for fourteen years between 1969 and 1984. While in office, he worked for equal treatment of all people. He also worked for better education and health care.

Rosa Parks, a black woman, got on a bus in Montgomery, Alabama, on December 1, 1955. The driver asked her to move to the back of the bus where all blacks were supposed to sit. She refused to do it. This began a 301-day *boycott* of Alabama busses by blacks. In the end, her courage led to more fair treatment of blacks throughout the country.

In Detroit, Parks has kept on with her work for minority rights. She has received the Martin Luther King, Jr., Non-Violent Peace Prize and many other honors. A street in Detroit has been named after her. A college *scholarship fund* in her honor has been set up for Michigan students who are good leaders.

For many years Rosa Parks has worked for equal rights for minorities.

Sojourner Truth was born a slave. She escaped from her owner and became free. She worked long and hard to improve the life of blacks before and during the Civil War.

Truth never learned to read or write. But she was a smart and friendly person. She lived her last days in Battle Creek. She is buried there in the Oak Hill Cemetery.

G. Mennen Williams served as governor of Michigan from 1949 to 1960. He was Chief Justice on the Michigan Supreme Court. He also was U.S. Secretary of State for African Affairs. During that time, Williams gathered many art pieces and artifacts. He gave them to the Detroit Institute of Arts.

Other political leaders:

John B. Swainson, Governor 1961-1962

George W. Romney, Governor 1963-1969

James J. Blanchard, Governor 1983-1990

G. Mennen Williams served as governor of Michigan from 1949 to 1960. Later he became Chief Justice of the Michigan Supreme Court.

Noteworthy People in the Arts

Harriette Simpson Arnow is a well-known author. She began writing when she was very young. Two of her stories take place in Michigan. One of them, *Hunter's Horn,* won the National Book Award in 1949. Another book, *The Dollmaker,* was made into a TV show. In this book Arnow tells the story of a poor rural family from the South who moved to Detroit to make a better life.

Gwen Frostic is a well-known artist, *poet,* and business woman. As a young child, she had polio. This was a sickness that paralyzed (PAIR-uh-lyzd) parts of her body. While getting over the sickness, she learned to make *block prints.* Frostic started a small mail-order business. She designed note paper, napkins, placemats, and postcards. Her ideas about nature are presented simply through words and art.

Frostic's studio is in Benzonia. Nearby, she has a 200-acre *wildlife sanctuary*. Wild animals and birds of many kinds live there in safety. Frostic has collected one of the biggest nature libraries in Michigan.

Eliel Saarinen, architect, designed Kingswood School at Cranbrook. He also founded the Cranbrook Academy of Arts in 1928. It is known world-wide as a center to train artists, architects, weavers, painters, and *sculptors*.

Gwen Frostic and her dog enjoy the land she writes about in her books.

The Cranbrook Academy of Art Museum is located in Bloomfield Hills. Carl Milles created the "Orpheus Fountain" which beautifies the grounds.

One of the *faculty* members, **Carl Milles,** was a sculptor. He created the beautiful fountain figures and other forms at Cranbrook.

Eliel Saarinen and his son, **Eero Saarinen,** designed and worked on the General Motors Technical Center in Warren. Eliel Saarinen died in 1950. His son completed the work on the center.

Minoru Yamasaki was a world-famous architect. He believed that when a person enters a building, "there should be *serenity* and delight." In his buildings, he tried to use materials other than glass and steel.

One of Yamasaki's buildings is the McGregor Conference Center at Wayne State University in Detroit.

Yamasaki never forgot his youth on the West Coast during World War II. During that war, Japan was an enemy of the United States. Because of this, there was much hate and prejudice against Japanese-Americans. Yamasaki was one of the thousands who were treated badly.

Noteworthy Entertainers

Diana Ross is a popular singer. She started out with the Supremes group. She became a top soloist. The Motown record company made many of the Supremes' hit records.

Berry Gordy, Jr., built Motown into a successful record company based on black music. He started out working in an automobile factory, writing songs part-time. Gordy also helped other black singers become big stars. The **Temptations** and

McGregor Memorial Conference Center at Wayne State University in Detroit. This building was designed by world-famous architect, Minoru Yamasaki.

Stevie Wonder are just two.

In 1972, because of the great success of Motown, the company moved to California.

Here are some other entertainers who started in Michigan:

Harry Boughton (Blackstone), magician

Aretha Franklin, singer

Julie Harris, actress

Alex Karras, actor and football player

Ed McMahon, announcer

George Peppard, actor

Lionel Richie, singer

George C. Scott, actor

Tom Selleck, actor

Actor Tom Selleck was born in Michigan.

Aretha Franklin also comes from Michigan.

Outstanding Scientists

Paul deKruif was an author and *microbiologist.* He wrote books about disease, hunger, and other forms of suffering throughout the world. He did much to raise standards of health care.

Dr. Pearl Kendrick and **Dr. Grace Eldering** developed a *vaccine* for whooping cough. 6,000 people were dying each year from whooping cough. Most of these deaths were young children. Over the years, this vaccine brought an end to whooping cough deaths.

Edward H. White II was the first astronaut to leave his spaceship while in outer space. The space walk lasted 21 minutes. Later, White died when a flash fire swept through the *Apollo* spacecraft at Cape Kennedy, Florida. **James McDivitt** made two space flights. One was with White. The other was with the first flight to the moon.

Outstanding Athletes

Joe Louis was a professional boxer. He held the world heavyweight championship for twelve years. Sportswriters called him the "Brown Bomber." He was a hero to millions of children across the country. Louis had a job in the Ford Motor Company but gave it up when he decided to box professionally.

It was a happy day in Michigan when the **Detroit Tigers** won the baseball World Series in 1984. Michigan has always been proud of its sports teams. Other sports heroes are:

Ty Cobb, baseball player   **Al Kaline,** baseball player
Thomas Hearns, boxer   **Billy Sims,** football player
Gordie Howe, hockey player   **Isiah Thomas,** basketball player

Joe Louis is remembered today as one of the best boxers of all time. He held the world heavyweight championship for twelve years.

Alan Trammell has been a Detroit Tiger for many years. Why is he regarded as a great player?

How many home runs did Cecil Fielder make during 1990?

Loyal fans cheer their favorite baseball team at the Tiger Stadium in Detroit.

Photo courtesy of the Detroit Tigers.

Isiah Thomas is an outstanding basketball player on the Detroit Pistons world championship team.

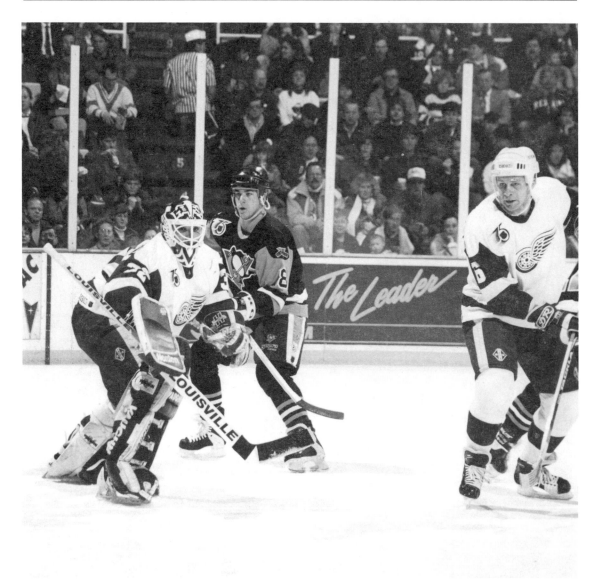

The Red Wings hockey team attracts many cheering fans.
Photo by John Hartman, courtesy Detroit Red Wings.

WORDS TO KNOW

STUDY

arts

journalist

serenity

block print

microbiologist

vaccine

boycott

scholarship fund

wildlife sanctuary

faculty

sculptor

WHAT DID YOU LEARN?

1. Why did Ralph Bunche receive the Nobel Peace Prize?

2. Who was the first woman lieutenant governor of Michigan?

3. Why was a street in Detroit named Rosa Parks Boulevard?

4. Who discovered the vaccine for whooping cough?

5. Who was the first astronaut to step outside the spaceship in outer space?

6. Why was Joe Louis a hero?

USING WHAT YOU HAVE LEARNED

1. Which three persons from this chapter would you most like to know? Why?

2. What are some common traits you think all these people have?

3. Who are the leading citizens in your community?

PROJECTS AND REPORTS

1. Interview a leading citizen in your community. Why do you think the person is outstanding? What kinds of activities does he or she do? Write a short report about the person's life and work. You might include a snapshot or draw a picture of the person.

2. Make a list of people in your town who you think are outstanding. Note their contributions. They may come from many different fields of work.

One interesting thing to do in Michigan is to visit Greenfield Village in Dearborn. There you can step into the past and enjoy the pleasures of earlier times.

Michigan: A Place to Enjoy

Summer Fun

Michigan offers many fun and interesting things to do. Summertime in Michigan means people can camp, fish, hike, bicycle, and golf. They can play tennis, swim, and boat.

Bird Watching

The Kirtland warbler is a small, yellow-breasted song bird. Each spring and summer it nests in northeastern Lower Michigan. It makes its nest in the young jack pine trees. It is the only bird which nests only within the borders of Michigan. Because of this, some people think it should become the state bird.

The bird is *endangered*. That means its numbers are getting fewer. The Kirtland warbler is *protected* by law. It is against the law to harm or catch one.

Taking Pictures

To photograph Michigan is enjoyable. Isle Royale, Tahquamenon Falls, Mackinac Island, and Greenfield Village offer lovely views for pictures. Michigan's wildlife are also very interesting

Almost everywhere in Michigan, beautiful scenery can be found. This is the Iroquois Hotel on Mackinac Island. Why do you think this hotel was given the name Iroquois?

subjects. Sometimes moose, whitetail deer, and black bear may *pose* for you in their own environment.

Winter Fun

There are many winter sports in our state. Ice fishing is popular with all ages. Tobogganing, ice skating, and snowmobiling are favorites with many people. People even come from other states to enjoy winter *pastimes*.

Ishpeming, in the Upper Peninsula, is a well-known ski center. Skiing began there in 1887 when three Norwegians

A winter hot dog roast.

Snowmobiling is a popular winter sport. What winter sports do you enjoy?

formed a ski club. A ski jumping championship takes place each year. Visitors to Ishpeming can also visit the National Ski Hall of Fame.

Iron Mountain, in the Upper Peninsula, is another ski hill. It has the world's highest manmade ski jump.

The Sand Dunes

Sleeping Bear Dunes National Lakeshore, near Glen Arbor, has the largest *dune* in the world. The name *Sleeping Bear* comes from a Chippewa story. A bear and her two cubs swam across Lake Michigan to escape a forest fire. The mother reached the shore safely and climbed on top of a hill. There she waited for her two cubs. She waited and waited, but they never arrived. The gods covered the waiting mother bear with sand. She became the Sleeping Bear Dune. The gods then raised the drowned cubs from the water and turned them into islands.

Festivals and Fairs

Hundreds of festivals are held in Michigan each year. Many towns, small and large, plan festivals. One of the biggest is the Cherry Festival held in Traverse City each July.

A few unusual events are held in Michigan. Stone skipping takes place on Mackinac Island. The International Cherry Pit Spitting Contest is held in Eau Claire. The Maple Syrup Festival is held in Shepherd and Vermontville each September. Some events attract hundreds of people. If you golf, it might be fun to join the "Polar Ice Cap Golf" during Grand Haven's Winterfest in February.

The Sleeping Bear Dune near Glen Arbor. Can you tell the Chippewa story about how this dune was formed?

Fort Michilimackinac presents a pageant and parade each year in May. The story of the pageant goes back to 1763 when Ottawa and Chippewa Indians took over the fort.

Michigan's biggest fair is the State Fair in Detroit. People prepare for this fair all year. Prizes are given for the best farm animals, cakes, and crafts, among other things. The contests, exhibits, and entertainment draw thousands of people.

Throughout Michigan, arts and crafts fairs are well-attended. Talented Michigan artists show and sell their works. The yearly Ann Arbor Art Fair draws a huge crowd each summer.

A fine collection of *folk art* is housed at Michigan State University. Fish and duck *decoys,* carvings, and quilts are only a few of the things to see there.

Michigan is proud of its "Artrain." It is the only art museum in the country that is housed on a train. It is a traveling museum. The train visits many towns. Artists on the train show how they do their art work.

Ethnic festivals are held all over the state. In Detroit, these take place during the summer. A different ethnic group

The Michigan State Fair in Detroit presents a magical scene at night.

"Artrain" is a five-car traveling museum that takes art and artists around the state on rails. The sides of the cars are painted with colorful murals. Has Artrain visited your town?

plans the program each week. The music, dances, foods, and costumes draw many people to the festivals. It is interesting to learn about the customs of others.

Saying YES to Michigan gives us many interesting experiences as we enjoy and learn more about our state and its people. Our own background becomes more broad as we discover new things.

WORDS TO KNOW

decoy

dune

endangered

folk art

pastime

pose

protected

STUDY

WHAT HAVE YOU LEARNED?

1. What bird is endangered in Michigan?

2. What are ten interesting things to do in our state?

PROJECTS AND REPORTS

1. Plan a session of bird watching near your school. Make a list of all the birds you see. Draw pictures of one or two kinds.

2. List three interesting things you would like to do to learn more about Michigan. Explain why you would like to do them. Share your list with your classmates.

3. Write a short report about an enjoyable trip you have taken, or would like to take, in Michigan.

4. Write a report about Michigan's Artrain. Try to make arrangements for the Artrain to visit your community. Contact the Michigan Council for the Arts.

These newsboys and girls are working for the Grand Rapids Press *in 1914.*
They are learning how to become useful citizens of Michigan.

Michigan in the Twenty-first Century

Y ou have read and studied about our state community throughout this book. It has helped you to understand your own background. You have read how people worked together to make your city or town a better place to live and work.

In a few years you will become an important citizen in your community. You will be paying taxes and voting for people of your choice. You will help decide what kind of city or town you want for the *future*.

Many important matters will need your attention. Public health, education, transportation, and *communication* are a few. Crime, jobs, conservation, energy, and peace are others.

Our choices will not only touch Michigan, but the world community. We have a chance to work together for a better world.

Change and the Future

There is a huge *mural* in the Garden Court at the Detroit Institute of Arts. This is a picture painted on a wall. It was painted by a world-famous artist, Diego Rivera.

The mural was finished in 1933. Before he painted it, Rivera visited Detroit. He studied the people, the factories, and many other buildings. The painting shows the automobile industry. It shows that human and natural resources have been used to make automobiles.

As one looks at the mural, one might wonder what Michigan will be like in the twenty-first *century*. (*Century* means 100 years. The twenty-first century starts with the year 2000.)

Activity – Town Mural

ACTIVITY

Suppose Rivera were asked to paint a picture of your community today. What do you think he would paint? What would seem important after he had visited your town and talked to the people? As a class, prepare a mural on roll paper. Show what you think your town is like.

Diego Rivera's mural at the Detroit Institute of Arts. What would a mural showing your city or town today look like?

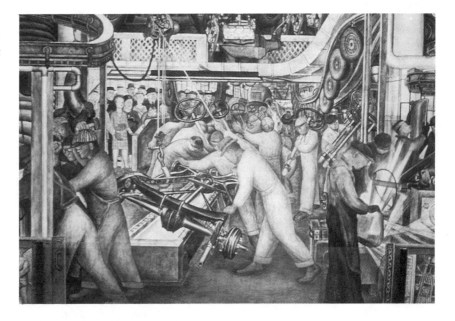

Trends in Michigan's History

A *trend* means something is heading in a general direction. If we look at trends from the past, these can direct our attention to thinking about the future.

- In the early 1900s, people began leaving the farms to work in the cities. With machinery to do the farm work, fewer farm workers were needed. There were plenty of automobile factories.

    The trend has been toward city jobs and away from farm work. Do you think there will be plenty of city jobs for everyone in the next century? Will new kinds of businesses come to

S. B. Nickels butcher shop in 1909. As people moved to the cities, they took jobs in factories or stores.

Parke, Davis & Co. plant. This company is still known world-wide for its drugs and medicines.

Michigan? Will people keep moving from the farms and to the suburbs? If so, what may happen to the farms?

• Thousands and thousands of people came to Michigan from other states and countries. They came to work in the factories. Immigrants were welcome because they were good workers. By working hard, a person could earn enough money to buy a home and an automobile.

The trend was toward a good standard of living for many people. Will Michigan still invite immigrants and people from other states? Will we have jobs, houses, schools, and health services for immigrants? Will people who work hard gain enough money to buy cars and houses?

• Henry Ford promised that he would pay workers at least a set minimum wage. He also said his factories would be open 24 hours a day.

The trend was toward better pay and plenty of jobs. Will there be good jobs for workers? Will people work 40 hours a week? Will pay keep getting better? What will people do with

These men and women are carrying food to strikers at the Fisher Body Plant in Flint.

their time off? How will they make a living if there are not enough jobs?

- In the 1930s and 1940s people formed unions. They worked to get better pay and safer work places.

  The trend was toward unions. How much power will unions have in the years ahead? Will they get stronger? Will they grow weaker?

- Black citizens showed their anger in the civil disturbances. They wanted a better life and to be treated fairly. This meant they wanted an end to race discrimination in jobs, housing, and education.

  The trend was toward equality for all people. Will blacks and other minorities be treated fairly? Will we ever be able to accept people without noticing the color of their skin?

ACTIVITY

POPULATION TRENDS

MICHIGAN'S POPULATION BY AGE

AGE GROUP	PERCENTAGE
Under 5 years	7%
5-13 years	14%
14-17 years	7%
18-24 years	13%
25-34 years	17%
35-44 years	12%
45-64 years	19%
65 and over	11%

Which age group has the greatest number of people? Which age group has the fewest people? How will these facts affect the future of Michigan? Will we need more or fewer school teachers? What percent of Michigan's population is 35 years and older?

Michigan's cities must plan to provide clean, safe places to live and jobs for their people. Cheboygan has recently restored its Opera House.

Houghton on a fall day.

Today in large Michigan cities, the population has been getting smaller. There is more crime. There are more empty buildings. Some factories and businesses have moved to other cities or states. How can our community become a safer and happier place to live? How can we invite new businesses to our state?

Some people are leaving Michigan for jobs in other states. The percentage of senior citizens is getting higher. There is a need to plan for these changes in Michigan's future.

POPULATION PROJECTIONS FOR MICHIGAN

ACTIVITY

YEAR	POPULATION
1980	9,258,000
1990	9,394,000
2000	9,208,000

If the projection comes true, will Michigan's population increase or decrease in the future? Can you think of any reasons for this?

The Gerber Co. in Fremont.

Longway Planetarium in Flint.

Changes in the world are affecting our state community. More foreign-made automobiles are being bought by Americans. For Michigan this means fewer automobiles will come out of the factories. Michigan has depended greatly on the automobile industry for its living.

It is clear to most people that there will be fewer jobs in the automobile factories. How will we handle this problem in our state?

Facing Hard Challenges

The questions that face us are hard ones. Citizens working together will bring us closer to answering the questions.

Changes are happening in space, transportation, medicine, energy, and other fields. The use of computers is already a part of your school studies. These changes have helped decide how we live. Changes lead us into the twenty-first century.

How you take part in your community will depend partly upon what you know of its past. Your community will depend on how you play your part as a citizen.

Abbott's Magic Co. of Colon provides jobs for some Michigan people. This company was started by Blackstone the Magician and his friend, Percy Abbott, an Australian magician.

The way we live is changing today. These students from Ann Arbor's Bryant Elementary School are learning how to use a computer.

Michigan's future will depend on how you play your part as a citizen.

STUDY

WORDS TO KNOW

century	mural
communication	trend
future	

WHAT HAVE YOU LEARNED?

1. Name four matters that will need attention in the future.

2. Who is Diego Rivera?

3. Name two trends, and tell how they will affect our life in the years ahead.

USING WHAT YOU HAVE LEARNED

1. What is a community?

2. In what kind of state community would you like to live? Why?

3. What do you feel are Michigan's strong points for meeting the needs of the years ahead?

PROJECTS AND REPORTS

1. Make a model of, or write about, an ideal community. What kinds of people would be living there? How would they be earning a living? What services would they need? In what kinds of homes would they be living? What kinds of transportation would they use?

2. Write a paper predicting your own future. Consider some of the following questions. Where will you be living? What kind of work will you be doing? What will you do for fun? There are many other questions you could discuss in the paper.

3. Make a chart to show what Michigan's strongest points are. Show how these will help in facing future challenges.

GOVERNORS OF THE STATE OF MICHIGAN

Stevens T. Mason 1835-1840	Hazen S. Pingree 1897-1900
William Woodbridge 1840-1841	Aaron T. Bliss 1901-1904
James Wright Gordon, Lieut. Gov..1841	Fred M. Warne 1905-1910
John S. Barry 1842-1846	Chase S. Osborn 1911-1912
Alpheus Felch 1846-1847	Woodbridge N. Ferris 1913-1916
William L. Greenly, Lieut. Gov. . . .1847	Albert E. Sleeper 1917-1920
Epaphroditus Ransom 1848-1850	Alexander J. Groesbeck 1921-1926
John S. Barry 1850-1851	Fred W. Green 1927-1930
Robert McClelland. 1852-1853	Wilber M. Brucker 1931-1932
Andrew Parsons, Lieut. Gov..1853-1854	William A. Comstock 1933-1934
Kinsley S. Bingham 1855-1858	Frank D. Fitzgerald 1935-1936
Moses Wisner 1859-1860	Frank Murphy 1937-1938
Austin Blair 1861-1864	Frank D. Fitzgerald 1939
Henry H. Crapo 1865-1868	Luren D. Dickinson 1939-1940
Henry P. Baldwin 1869-1872	Murray D. Van Wagoner 1941-1942
John J. Bagley 1873-1876	Harry F. Kelly 1943-1946
Charles M. Croswell 1877-1880	Kim Sigler 1947-1948
David H. Jerome 1881-1882	G. Mennen Williams 1949-1960
Josiah W. Begole 1883-1884	John B. Swainson 1961-1962
Russell A. Alger 1885-1886	George Romney 1963-1969
Cyrus G. Luce 1887-1890	William G. Milliken 1969-1982
Edwin B. Winans 1891-1892	James J. Blanchard 1983-1990
John T. Rich 1893-1896	John Engler 1991-

Glossary

abolitionist (a-boh-LIH-shun-ust) a person who wants to end slavery

absentee ballot a ballot voters may use if they are unable to go to the voting place on election day

acid rain certain chemicals in the air which may cause harm to living things

advantage something extra or good which will be helpful in a certain way

agriculture (AG-rih-kul-cher) farming; raising crops and animals for food and for sale

amendment (uh-MEND-munt) a change added to improve a law

ancestor (AN-ses-ter) a person from whom someone is descended, such as a grandparent or great-grandparent

anthropologist (an-thro-PAHL-uh-jist) a person who studies early people and their way of life

anti- a prefix meaning opposite or against; anti-slavery means having feelings against owning slaves

appliance a small machine that does a certain job, such as a toaster or electric can opener

applique (AP-luh-kay) a decoration cut from one piece of material and sewn or pasted onto another piece of material

archaeologist (ar-kee-AHL-uh-jist) a person who studies how people lived long ago by digging up and examining tools, weapons, dishes, fossils, and other artifacts

artifact anything made by people in the past, especially tools and weapons

arts painting, drawing, sculpture, poetry, dancing, music, literature

assembly line in a factory, an arrangement of workers so that each person does a certain task as the product passes by

bateaux (bah-TOH) (French) a lightweight, flat-bottomed river boat

bilingual (by-LIN-gwul) speaking two different languages

biracial (by-RAY-shul) belonging to or having two different races

bill written idea for a new law

block print a design or picture made by coating a cut-out block of wood with ink or paint and pressing it on a piece of paper or cloth

board of education a group of people elected to run the schools in a district

bobsled a long sled with steering equipment and brakes

booming moving a large group of logs down the river

border the line that divides one place from another, such as between countries and states

boulder a huge rock that is rounded and smooth

boundary something that shows a limit or end; a dividing line

bow the front end of a boat

boycott to refuse to buy or use a product or service

brine water containing a great deal of salt

bulk of great size; a large amount

buoy (BOY) a floating object anchored in the water to warn ships of dangerous rocks or sand bars

burial mound a pile of dirt built over a grave, especially by early Native Americans

calumet (KAL-uh-met) a long-stemmed pipe smoked as a sign of peace

candidate (KAN-dih-dut) a person who is running for office

cargo goods carried by a ship or other vehicle

carriage (KAR-eej) a wheeled vehicle for carrying persons or a load; sometimes pulled by horses

catalog (KAT-uh-log) a list of things that can be bought

cemetery a place for burying the dead

century (SEN-cher-ee) a period of one hundred years

ceremony (SAIR-uh-mohn-ee) an act or series of acts done in a particular order by custom

channel a deep, narrow course through which water flows

chemical a substance formed when two or more other substances act upon one another

civilized (SIV-ul-yzd) educated; advanced in social organization, arts, and sciences

clan a group of families who have the same ancestors

climate (KLY-mut) the average weather of a place over several years

collective bargaining (kuh-LEK-tiv BAR-gun-eeng) a way to settle a dispute by each side giving in a little until they reach an agreement

commercial (kuh-MER-shul) having to do with the buying and selling of goods, especially on a large scale

communication (kuh-myew-nih-KAY-shun) the exchange of information between persons in all kinds of ways

community college a small college offering only the first two years of courses

community a group of people living in a particular place; the area itself

compete to try to win the same thing that someone else is trying to win

compulsory (kom-PUL-suh-ree) being required by law or rules

conductor a person on the Underground Railroad who helped slaves escape to freedom

conserve (kon-SERV) to keep and protect

consolidated (kon-SAHL-ih-day-tud) joined together

constitution (kon-stih-TOO-shun) the rules used to govern a state, country, or social group

construction the act of building something

continent (KAHN-tih-nent) one of the earth's seven large bodies of land

contribution something that is given or shared, such as an idea or money

convention a group of people gathered together for a common purpose

conveyor belt (kon-VAY-er belt) a wide belt, connected with moving wheels or rollers, used to carry things from one place to another

cooperation (koh-opp-er-AY-shun) working well together

coroner (KOR-uh-ner) a public official whose job is to find out the cause of death when not by natural causes

county government that level of government which is just below the state; county government often carries out state laws and plans

crew a group of people who work together on a ship, airplane, or train

crusader (krew-SAY-der) a person who works eagerly to improve conditions

customs certain ways of doing things among a group of people

cylinder (SIL-un-der) a long, round object, either hollow or solid; a cylinder is used in the engine of an automobile

debate talk or argument about a question in which both sides are presented

decoy a model of a bird used by hunters to attract real birds

decrease to become less

degree a series of steps by which something is measured

democratic believing or practicing the idea that people are equal; a kind of government in which the highest power is held by the people and exercised through representatives

deposit large amount of minerals in rock or in the ground

depression a time of slow business activity when many people are out of work

descendant one who comes down from a particular ancestor

desert to leave a person or thing that one should stay with

diet the food and drink that a person or animal usually takes

dirt farmer a farmer who works his own land

discrimination (dis-krim-ih-NAY-shun) treating someone unfairly because of the person's difference from other people

disease illness, sickness

dispute a disagreement or argument

dune hill of sand piled up by wind

education schooling, knowledge about all kinds of ideas and things

electric screen a screen that is electrically charged so it shocks a person or thing which touches it

elevation height above sea level, as in the height of land

endangered in an unsafe condition; usually meaning a kind of animal is at risk of being completely destroyed

equator an imaginary line which is halfway between the North Pole and South Pole

ethnic having to do with a race or a group of people who share a common background and customs

exaggerate (eg-ZA-jer-ayt) to make something seem larger or greater than it is

executive (eg-ZEK-yew-tiv) a person who is the head of a government or business

expedition a trip made for a special reason, such as exploring unknown lands

explorer a traveler searching for new information about the area

faculty (FA-kul-tee) all the teachers of a school or college

federal having to do with the government in Washington, D.C.

fell to cut down trees

ferry a boat carrying people and cargo over water

fertile (FER-tul) able to grow many crops and plants

Fish Commission a group of people selected to work on the problems of fishing in the state

folk art art, music, dance, and stories of the common people

food processing canning, freezing, drying, and other things done to save food for later use

fossil hardened remains of plants, animals, and shells that were buried in the earth long ago

founder a person who begins a company or school

freedom being able to move about, speak, and act according to one's own will; not being controlled by others

freight (FRAYT) goods hauled by land, air, or water

future time that has yet to come

geographer person who studies the surface of the earth and the plants, animals, and people on it

geologist person who studies the history of the earth by examining rocks and minerals

ghost town the remains of a town where people had lived

glacier (GLAY-shur) a large mass of ice which moves slowly across the land

globe a round ball shape with a map of the world on it; a model of the earth

handicraft things made with one's hands, such as pottery and hand-sewn items

hardwood strong, heavy wood of trees with broad leaves, such as oak and maple

hatchery a place for hatching eggs of fish or chickens

highland games games held by Scottish people, usually including track and field events, tossing games, highland dancing, and bagpipe playing

historian person who studies and writes about the past

historic having to do with history; famous in history

human resources people who can think of the ideas and do the work of life

immigrant person who comes from one country to live in another country

income tax money paid to a government based on one's earnings

independent free from rule or control of another person or country

industrialize (in-DUS-tree-ul-yz) to develop factories, machines, and manufacturing activities

industry manufacturing and business activity

inquisitive (in-KWIZ-ih-tiv) being curious; eager to ask questions

interest money paid by a borrower for the use of borrowed money

internal combustion engine a motor that works by the burning of gasoline within it to produce power

international between or affecting two or more countries

interview to meet with and ask questions of another person to gain information

invention something created for the first time

inventor one who thinks up and makes new things

invest to place money in a business in order to earn more money

isolate (I-so-layt) to separate or keep apart from others

issue a matter in dispute

journalist (JER-nul-ist) one who writes for a newspaper or magazine

judicial (jew-DISH-ul) having to do with courts and judges

latitude distance north and south of the equator measured in degrees

legend a list of symbols or colors on a map and what they stand for

legislative having the power or authority to make laws

license (LY-suns) a paper giving legal permission for a person to do or have something

life preserver a belt, round tube, or jacket which keeps a person floating in water

lock a part of a canal in which the water level can be changed to raise or lower ships

longitude distance east or west from a line drawn between the North and South poles and running through Greenwich, England

lumbering the business of cutting logs

lumberjack a person who cuts down trees and prepares logs for the sawmill

magnesium a silver-white light metal used in photography and in manufacturing.

magnetic compass an instrument for showing directions by means of a magnetic needle that points north

majority an amount greater than half the total

manufacturing (man-uh-FAK-chereeng) making something from raw materials by machinery

mass transit public transportation for large numbers of people

mechanic (meh-KAN-ik) one who builds and repairs machines

metropolitan (met-roh-PAHL-ih-tun) having to do with a large or important city

microbiologist one who studies about small plants and bacteria, usually with the aid of a microscope

migrant a farm worker who travels from place to place to harvest seasonal crops

militia (muh-LIH-shuh) army made up of citizens who fight or help out in emergencies

mineral certain things found under the ground which are for human use, such as copper and iron

minimum the lowest amount needed, possible, or allowed

minority (my-NOR-ih-tee) less than half of a whole group; part of a population that is different from other groups in some ways and is sometimes discriminated against

misbehavior improper, rude, or bad behavior; acting in these ways

mission special job or task

missionary one sent to spread a religious faith among unbelievers

model a person who sets a good example; a small but exact copy of something

mortgage (MOR-geej) giving property as a guarantee that borrowed money will be paid back

mosque (MAHSK) building used by Moslems for worship

motto (MAH-toh) a short statement that says what someone believes or what something stands for

municipal (myew-NIH-sih-pul) having to do with a city or town

mural a picture painted on a wall or ceiling

nation people connected by common language, customs, or government; country

native a person born in a particular place or country; one of the original inhabitants of a place

native-born a person born in a certain place or country

natural resources things in nature that may be used by people to make life more comfortable

nursery a place where young plants, flowers, and trees are grown and usually sold

oral history collection of memories of living people about their past experiences

ordinance a law passed by a city or village

overproduce to make or grow more than is needed

pastime something that makes time pass pleasantly

pedestrian a person who travels on foot

peninsula a piece of land extending out into a body of water

pension a fixed amount of money paid regularly to a retired person

physician a doctor who treats sickness or injury

piñata (peen-YAH-tuh) hollow animal or other shape made from clay or paper, usually filled with toys and candy.

pit a hole in the ground

plant fish to place fish from a hatchery into lakes and rivers to grow

populate to furnish with people

population the number of people who live in a place

port a place along the shore where boats and ships can anchor and be safe from storms

pose to stay in one position for picture taking

prejudice (PREH-jew-dis) a favoring or dislike of one over another without good reason, facts, or careful thought

preserve to prepare food so that it will not spoil; to save or protect

prime meridian the imaginary line that runs from the North Pole to the South Pole through Greenwich, England; the starting point for measuring longitude

private belonging to a particular group or person, not government

private property property such as land belonging to a particular person or group

privilege a right or opportunity given to a person or group

process a number of things that are done in making or doing something

product something that is made or grown

professional having to do with a job that is not mechanical or agricultural and that requires special education

profit the money left over after all the bills are paid in a business or company

property tax a tax paid on land, buildings or automobiles

protected defended; kept from harm

province one of the parts that Canada is divided into, like a state

publish to print and sell books, magazines, or newspapers

quadricycle a vehicle like a motorcycle but having four wheels

radar an instrument used to find and track distant objects by the use of radio waves

reception the act or manner of welcoming and receiving people

refinery a place where oil or metals are made pure

refrigeration being made or kept cool

refugee (REF-yew-jee) a person who flees for safety, especially to another country

register to write in a list or record, as to register an automobile or to register to vote

rehabilitation (ree-huh-bil-ih-TAY-shun) the act of restoring a person to a state of health; preparing a handicapped person to get along in society or to hold a job

relief the money, clothes, or food given to help ease the pain and worry of being without

represent to stand for something; to act for or in place of

representative one who is selected to speak or act for others

reputation the way others think about a person

reservation land set aside by the government for a special purpose, such as a place for Native Americans to live

resource a usable stock or supply, as of water or coal

responsible expected to answer or account for something

responsibility the condition of being accountable for a task

restore to bring something back to the way it was earlier; bring to a better state

revenue (REV-uh-new) money that a business, person, or government takes in

riot a public fight by a crowd of people

rural having to do with living in the country rather than the city

sales tax a tax on the sale of property and goods; a tax paid by the person who buys something

saline (SAY-leen) containing salt

sanitarium a place people go to for rest or relaxation if they are ill

sapling a young tree

scale a way of showing size or distance on a map in relation to the real thing

scenic (SEE-nik) giving views of natural scenery such as hills and lakes

scholarship gift of money to help a student pay for his or her education

scholarship fund money collected and used to help students with the expenses of education

sculptor a person who makes statues by carving or modeling, as in clay, wood, or metal

seal a design placed on a letter or document to show that it is official

section a division of land equal to one square mile

self-sufficient being able to get along without help from others

serenity being quiet and calm

shale a fine-grained rock formed from hardened clay

similarity likeness or resemblance

slavery being owned or in bondage to someone

social scientist one who studies people and how they live and work together in groups

solar compass an instrument showing directions by the use of energy from the sun

spawning grounds places where fish, frogs and other water animals produce or plant their eggs

specialize (SPESH-ul-yz) to limit one's energy to one business or subject; in farming, to grow mostly one crop

state of emergency a condition when a threatening event happens without warning and calls for quick action

state school fund money collected and used for public schools

station a stopping place along a road or trail

steamer a boat moved by steam

stern the rear part of a boat or ship

stock the amount of money or other capital invested in a large business; a share of ownership in a company

strait a narrow channel between two bodies of water

strike a work stoppage by workers to force an employer to meet their demands

substitute to use one thing in place of another

surrender to give up

surveyor (ser-VAY-er) a person who measures land to find out its boundaries, shape, and size

suspension bridge a bridge which hangs from cables stretched between towers

symbol (SIM-bul) a sign or mark used to stand for the real thing, as a dot on a map stands for a city

tan to change a hide into leather by soaking it in chemicals

territory any large area of land; a region

timber growing trees that may be cut for their wood; wood that may be used to make something

township an area of land six miles square; a local unit of government

trading post a store in a place where there are few people; where goods may be bought and sold

tradition customs and beliefs that are passed down from parents to their children

traditional handed down from age to age

trans- (prefix) across to the other side

transportation means of carrying or moving people and things from one place to another

treaty an agreement made by negotiation between two or more countries

trend general direction or course taken

tuition (too-IH-shun) money paid by a student to attend school

Underground Railroad a network of paths, people, and buildings by which slaves escaped to freedom

unguarded border a line between two countries that people may pass over freely, with little questioning

union (YEW-nyun) a group of workers organized to protect their rights and jobs

unite to join together in one group

urban having to do with a city or city life

utility a business providing a public service and which must obey special government rules; for example water, gas, or electric companies

vaccine (vak-SEEN) medication of weak germs used to protect people against certain diseases

vegetarian (vej-uh-TAIR-ee-un) a person who eats only plants and plant products (who eats no meat)

veto (VEE-toh) the power of a chief executive, such as the governor or president, to refuse to sign a bill into law

vocation a career or job

volunteer a person who offers to help or work without pay

voyageur a person hired by a fur company to transport goods and men by boat to trading posts

wampum small shell beads used as money and jewelry by the Indians

whaleback a sailing vessel for carrying ore

wigwam a shelter made of poles covered with bark, leaves, or hides

wildlife sanctuary (SANK-chew-air-ee) a place where wild animals are protected

Acknowledgments

Special thanks to the following educators for reviewing the manuscript of this text and making valuable suggestions for changes: Dr. John Chapman, Michigan Dept. of Education; Dr. Louise Frazier and Dr. Norman MacRae, Detroit Public Schools; Dr. Diana Umstattd, Saginaw; Vickie Weiss, Grand Blanc; Jean Prough, Flickinger Elementary School, Utica; Debra Schostak, Southfield; Barbara Duncan, Crary School, Lathrup Village.

Appreciation is expressed to Evelyn Kachaturoff, Shirley Tolan, and to all my colleagues — teachers who have contributed ideas, reviewed the manuscript, and permitted me to visit their fourth grade classrooms.

The author wishes to express special acknowledgment to Madge Baird for her editorial assistance. Also, appreciation is extended to Catherine W. Smith, editor, and others involved in the production of this textbook.

The author also wishes to express appreciation to the personnel of libraries, particularly the Library at the University of Michigan-Dearborn, the West Bloomfield Library, and the State of Michigan Archives, and to the many others who provided research materials and photographs. The Michigan State Department of Education was extremely helpful in providing information, as were the many other state and municipal agencies and departments throughout the state. The author wishes to thank the many other individuals and public and private organizations who contributed information and photographs for this publication.

Photograph Credits

Letters beside the numbers designate position on the page: T (top), M (middle), B (bottom), L (left), R (right).

Alpena Chamber of Commerce, 193L

Artrain, 266B

Caxton Printers (Caldwell, Idaho). From *Tall Timber Tales,* by Dell J. McCormick (1956) p.120, 107

Chandlee, Esme (Los Angeles), 255L

Cheboygan Industrial Development Corp. brochure, 27

Detroit, City of, 75, 204, 208, 212, 231, 236, 270

Detroit News, 246, 250 255R

Detroit Tigers, 257

Environmental Research Institute of Michigan, vi

Flint Convention and Visitors Bureau, 171, 275

Ford Motor Co., Technical and Regulatory Public Affairs Dept., 170, 172

Frostic, Gwen, 252

Greenfield Village and Henry Ford Museum, 38, 134, 167, 178T, 220, 224

Index